The Soviet Withdrawal from Afghanistan

Nearly ten years of bloodshed and political turmoil have followed the Soviet invasion of Afghanistan in 1979. Soviet occupation not only proved a major trauma for the people of Afghanistan; invasion ended at a stroke the growth in superpower detente that had characterised the late 1970s; and back at home in the Soviet Union the effects of escalating military costs and over 13,000 young military casualties have been felt at every level of society.

The decision to withdraw combat forces under the provisions of the Geneva Accords of April 1988 is one of the most dramatic developments in the international system since the end of the Second World War. Unable to overcome fierce insurgent *Mujahideen* resistance, the new Soviet leadership, under General Secretary Gorbachev, has opted to cut its military losses under a veil of UN diplomacy. The effects of this decision will be felt not only in Afghanistan, but in the Soviet Union, in Southwest Asia, and in the wider world.

The Soviet Withdrawal from Afghanistan has been designed to explore the background to the decision to withdraw and its broader implications. The authors, all established specialists, examine the Geneva Accords; the future for post-withdrawal Afghanistan; and the impact of withdrawal on regional states, Soviet foreign and domestic policies, the Soviet armed forces, Sino-Soviet relations and world politics. They write from diverse disciplinary traditions, while bringing together a shared sensitivity to the issues which complicate the Afghan question.

The Soviet Withdrawal from Afghanistan

edited by

Amin Saikal
Australian National University, Canberra

and

William Maley
University of New South Wales, Kensington

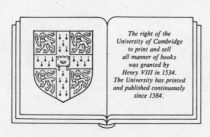

The right of the
University of Cambridge
to print and sell
all manner of books
was granted by
Henry VIII in 1534.
The University has printed
and published continuously
since 1584.

Cambridge University Press

Cambridge
New York   Port Chester
Melbourne   Sydney

Published by the Press Syndicate of the University of Cambridge
The Pitt Building, Trumpington Street, Cambridge CB2 1RP
32 East 57th Street, New York, NY 10022, USA
10 Stamford Road, Oakleigh, Melbourne 3166, Australia

First published 1989

Printed in Great Britain at the University Press, Cambridge

British Library Cataloguing in Publication data applied for

Library of Congress Cataloging in Publication data applied for

ISBN 0 521 37577 0 hard covers
ISBN 0 521 37588 6 paperback

For all the innocent victims of the Afghan War

All royalties from the publication of *The Soviet Withdrawal from Afghanistan* are being paid to Save the Children to assist with their Afghan projects

Contents

Preface

This book grew out of an international symposium held on 19 August 1988 by the Department of Political Science, Faculty of Arts, Australian National University. The symposium was opened by the Australian Defence Minister, The Honourable K.C. Beazley, M.P., who made time in a busy schedule to contribute a thoughtful address on Australian Government perspectives on Soviet withdrawal from Afghanistan. The Vice-Chancellor of the Australian National University, Professor L.W. Nichol, kindly chaired the opening session. The contributors to the symposium were asked to prepare papers on specified aspects of the Soviet withdrawal from Afghanistan which fell within their individual areas of expertise. Beyond this, they were in no way obliged to adopt a particular methodological approach, or to conform to a particular line of argument. This volume contains revised versions of the papers which were presented at the symposium, together with an introductory essay by the editors.

We owe sincere thanks not only to Mr Beazley, Professor Nichol, and the contributors, but to several other people who played key roles in making the symposium possible. Most of all our thanks go to the Head of the Department of Political Science, Professor Nancy Viviani, whose enthusiasm and support for this project were boundless. We are also indebted to Dr Robert Cushing, Dean of the Faculty of Arts, for generously making funds available to support the symposium, and for his encouragement. Sharon Merten showed great organisational skill and personal patience, ably backed by Thelma Wasiliew. For their great help in arranging the symposium, we warmly thank them both. Mary-Louise Hickey has been a constant source of support throughout the duration of this project, and proof-read the manuscript with meticulous care.

Finally, we must thank the staff of the Department of Politics, University College, University of New South Wales, in which the manuscript of this book was assembled. Professor Ian McAllister provided moral support. Alvaro Ascui and David W. Lovell gave generously of their time to supply advice on word-processing. Shirley Ramsay and Beverley Lincoln typed many difficult pages with great good cheer. We thank them all.

Amin Saikal
William Maley

Canberra
January 1989

1

Introduction

Amin Saikal and William Maley

After nearly a decade of bloodshed and political turmoil following the Soviet invasion of Afghanistan in late December 1979, the withdrawal of Soviet combat forces from Afghanistan brings to an end the only episode of sustained foreign occupation in the country's modern history. The introduction of Soviet forces *en masse* resulted not simply in an unprecedented trauma for Afghanistan, but in a regional and global crisis which in a very real sense snuffed out the *détente* between the Superpowers which had developed in fits and starts from at least the late 1960s.[1] An end to the Soviet involvement in Afghanistan is a momentous development on two different levels. The people of Afghanistan have borne the brunt of Soviet military activities, and an evacuation of Soviet troops is for them an occurrence of singular importance. But they are by no means the only actors to have felt the impact of the war. Other regional states have been forced to adjust to the Soviet presence, and this has influenced their domestic political structures and their relations with each other. The Soviet Union has been affected in manifold ways. And even at the global level, the Afghan crisis has impinged on the international relations of the USSR. The purpose of this book is to examine the more important consequences of Soviet withdrawal from Afghanistan.

1

The Geneva Accords on Afghanistan of 14 April 1988, concluded under the auspices of the United Nations between the Soviet-backed communist regime of the People's Democratic Party of Afghanistan (PDPA) and the Government of Pakistan, and jointly guaranteed by the Soviet Union and the United States, provided the overall framework for the Soviet withdrawal. They met with widespread international approval, and also delivered a diplomatic triumph for the United Nations, which for some time prior had been under mounting criticism for extravagance and inefficiency.

Yet the Geneva Accords could at best furnish a starting point for a comprehensive settlement to what is an exceptionally complicated problem. They did not provide for transition to a legitimate government in Afghanistan based on the claim of Afghans to determine their own future free of outside interference—and thus they left one of the key elements of the Afghan problem unresolved. None the less, as Soviet troops were withdrawn through 1988, the further weakening of the Kabul regime[2] ultimately prompted an exasperated Soviet leadership to commence direct talks with the Afghan Islamic resistance forces (*Mujahideen*)—thereby meeting a longstanding resistance demand. In early December, Soviet Deputy Foreign Minister and Ambassador to Kabul Iu.M. Vorontsov met in Taif, Saudi Arabia, with a *Mujahideen* delegation headed by Professor Burhanuddin Rabbani. These discussions have opened new avenues through which a viable settlement may ultimately be procured.

Afghanistan is indeed a very complex political unit. The Afghan crisis of the last decade finds its roots in this complexity. Whilst the external boundaries of the Afghan state had largely been settled by the end of the nineteenth century, the degree of control exercised over its territory by the central state administration remained comparatively feeble.[3] Afghan society has been marked by sharp divisions on ethnic, linguistic, tribal, and even sectarian lines, and between country and city. The cleavage between the important tribally-organised Pushtuns and the rest of the population (also split into a number of different groups) has always been sharp. Amongst the Pushtuns, tribal rivalries have frequently been intense. Furthermore, whilst the overwhelming majority of Afghans are Sunni Muslims, a significant minority, of 15-20%, are adherents of the heterodox

2

Shi'ite sect. The most important units of social organisation have historically been tribal or local, with political and economic interactions based on Islamic and customary law, rather than on decrees from the capital. Kabul remained remote and relatively unimportant.

When the central state intruded upon the prerogatives of important non-state actors, a clash could quickly develop. This happened in 1928-1929, when the reformist King Amanullah, who had succeeded in securing Afghanistan's sovereignty in foreign as well as domestic affairs, was overthrown in a revolt led by a Tajik bandit known as *Bacha-i Saqao* ('The Son of the Water Carrier').[4] The rule of the *Bacha* lasted only a matter of months, and he was displaced with relative ease by General Nadir Khan, a prominent Pushtun with royal connections. Nadir was assassinated in November 1933, and his throne went to his nineteen-year-old son, Mohammad Zahir. The new king understandably showed no inclination to rock the boat. For nearly thirty years, he left the running of the country first to his two uncles (1933-1953) and then to his cousin and brother-in-law Mohammad Daoud, Prime Minister from 1953-1963, and, following a 1973 coup against the King, President of the short-lived Afghan Republic until the April 1978 PDPA coup. Kabul's interventions in the countryside throughout this period of extended stability were as a rule carefully planned, and the clash of 1928-1929 was not repeated. But paradoxically, the contentment of the countryside with Kabul's behaviour disguised the fact that forces were developing in the capital which had the capacity to overthrow the government, even though they had no basis on which to secure the loyalty of the powerful rural population.

The most important of these forces was the small, factionalised, but strategically-placed communist movement. In the mid-1950s, Daoud was eager to embark on a limited process of state-building for which, however, he needed outside financial backing and arms. This was not forthcoming from the United States. Daoud's need for arms sprang in part from a border dispute with Pakistan—and as the US was at the time allied to Pakistan, its response was to advise Daoud to resolve the dispute by diplomatic means.[5] This drove Daoud into the hands of the post-Stalin leadership of the Soviet Union, which was seeking to counterbalance American penetration of the region. As a result, the USSR embarked upon a generous process of economic and military aid,[6] as it did also for India, another non-aligned regional state in dispute with Pakistan. This aid was sufficient to give the Soviet Union a very strong infrastructure of influence in Afghanistan. In particular, the Soviet Union was assiduous in cultivating radical elements in the tiny Afghan intelligentsia, and in building support for the USSR amongst largely de-tribalised youth sent to the Soviet Union for military training. The eventual result was the emergence by the mid-1960s of two minute but well-positioned pro-Soviet factions, the *Khalq* ('Masses') group led by Nur Mohammad Taraki and Hafizullah Amin, and the *Parcham* ('Banner') group headed by Babrak Karmal. From the very beginning, relations between these two groups were tense, in part due to their different social constituencies, but also because of hostility between their leaders. The *Khalq* was dominated largely by Pushtuns of rural origin, whereas the *Parcham* derived backing mainly from urbanised speakers of Dari (a dialect of Persian). In 1965, the factions were organisationally united in the PDPA, but in 1967 the party split, and it was only in 1977, under Soviet pressure, that it re-formed.[7]

The remoteness of these factions from Afghan society can hardly be overemphasised. Yet in the hot house of court politics, especially during the liberal climate of the 'constitutional period' following Daoud's resignation in 1963, they were able to play a larger role than their size merited. And a tactical alliance between Daoud and the *Parcham* faction, informally approved by the Soviet leadership, was crucial in triggering the July 1973 coup against the monarchy.[8] *Parcham*'s joy of course was short-lived, as Daoud moved to rid himself of those *Parchamis* and *Parcham* supporters who figured in his first republican Cabinet; and in some ways sought to distance himself from the Soviet Union.[9] By 1978, Daoud appeared untrustworthy to both the Soviet leadership and the communists in Kabul. Thus, when he moved to crack down on the PDPA leaders following a large public demonstration in April 1978, there was little to deter his opponents from attempting a coup. *Parchamis* in the Soviet-trained-and-equipped Afghan Air Force and Tank Brigade had little difficulty in liquidating Daoud and most of his immediate associates. Within a matter of days, the PDPA leaders announced the establishment of the 'Democratic Republic of Afghanistan', to which the Soviet Government immediately pledged its full support. Nur Mohammad Taraki was appointed President and Prime Minister, with Karmal and Amin each serving as Deputy Prime Minister.

The cleavage between the PDPA and the bulk of Afghan society sabotaged its attempts to consolidate its rule, despite extensive Soviet support, confirmed in a Treaty of Friendship between the regime and Moscow signed in December 1978. Its policies—including ill-considered 'land reform' proposals and decrees on the status of women[10]—were from the point of view of most Afghans not only unnecessary and provocative but repulsively anti-Islamic. Combined with the insensitivity of cadrés charged with imposing the new policies, this prompted a series of rural uprisings, which began in late 1978 and spread swiftly in spring and summer of 1979. The regime was in no position to deal effectively with this opposition, for it had rapidly been rent by the resurfacing of the old split between the *Khalq* and *Parcham*. Karmal and his associates were first sent abroad on diplomatic postings, and then expelled from the party in their absence. At this point, most headed for Moscow. Yet even within the *Khalq* faction, unity could not be maintained. In September 1979, the Soviet leadership plotted with Taraki to remove Amin, Prime Minister since March of that year and the firmest proponent of radical change through mass terror, and to replace him with Karmal. The Soviet leadership had always preferred Karmal and his faction, which they saw as both more sophisticated politically and more reliable ideologically. However, the plot miscarried disastrously; Taraki was eliminated by Amin, who replaced him as President and leader of the PDPA. This, and the deteriorating military situation in Afghanistan, confronted the Soviet leadership with a considerable dilemma—whether to intervene to save a collapsing Soviet-backed regime, or to let it collapse, with all the implications that such a collapse would carry for Soviet interests not only in Afghanistan but elsewhere in the world. The Soviets decisively resolved this dilemma when they despatched their invasion force to Afghanistan in late December 1979, killing Amin, replacing him with Karmal and citing the 1978 Treaty in defence of their action.[11]

Any hopes the Soviets may have entertained for a swift victory were quickly confounded. Rather than suppressing popular opposition to the regime, the introduction of Soviet forces boosted it. The use of terror against the civilian population, far from undermining the determination of the opposition, simply fuelled hatred of the invaders and their surrogates.[12] Resistance, which to that point had largely been localised, took a national character, focused on the Islamic forces known as *Mujahideen*. Resistance political parties, which previously had attracted little attention, became conduits for the supply to affiliated field commanders of military aid sent by states affronted by the Soviet invasion. Of these, the most important proved to be Egypt, Saudi Arabia, Iran, China and the United States—not to mention Pakistan, which not only provided haven for a population of Afghan refugees which by 1988 came to number over three million, but also facilitated the flow of arms to the *Mujahideen*, and housed the headquarters of the seven most important Sunni resistance parties.

These parties, while all Islamic, reflected the influence of different strands of thought within Islam. Four were touched by radical ideas which had developed in other parts of the Islamic world,[13] although in varying ways. These were the *Hezb-i Islami* (Islamic Party) of Gulbuddin Hekmatyar, a party of the same name led by Yunis Khalis, the *Jamiat-i Islami* (Islamic Society) headed by Professor Burhanuddin Rabbani, and a very small organisation, the *Ittehad-i Islami* (Islamic Alliance) of Professor Abdul Rasul Sayyaf. Of these, Rabbani's developed into the best-organised and most moderate. A further three displayed the influence of democratic tendencies within the framework of traditional Afghan Islam, and were at one in championing the claim that former King Mohammad Zahir, living in exile in Rome, could play a constructive role in resolving the Afghan crisis. These were the *Harakat-i Enqilab-i Islami* (Islamic Revolutionary Movement) of Mohammad Nabi Mohammadi; the *Jabhe-i Najad-i Melli* (National Liberation Front) of Professor Sibghatullah Mojaddedi; and the *Mahaz-i Islami* (Islamic Front) of Ahmad Gailani. Relations between these various parties were often poor, with Hekmatyar seen as particularly ambitious and obstreperous. None the less, these parties managed to form a loose coalition in May 1985 under the title of *Islamic Unity of Afghan Mujahideen*. While this alliance excluded a number of Shi'ite parties based either in Afghanistan or Iran, it brought together the parties whose field commanders would be crucial to a viable settlement of the Afghan problem.[14]

The activities of these field commanders were instrumental in creating the Kremlin's post-invasion dilemmas.[15] By their determined armed resistance, augmented from mid-1986 by the supply from Western countries of Stinger and Blowpipe anti-aircraft missiles, they succeeded—despite their relative lack of unity—in denying the Soviet Union the *political* objectives which underpinned the invasion. This, together with the palpable weakness of the Kabul regime even after the replacement of Karmal by his fellow *Parchami* Dr Najibullah in May 1986, finally prompted a new Soviet leadership generation under General Secretary Mikhail Gorbachev to use the veil of a 'negotiated settlement' as cover for a Soviet retreat.

The way in which this was managed is examined in William Maley's chapter. His concern is to explain the origins of the Geneva negotiating process from which the April 1988 Accords issued, to identify the main provisions of the Accords, and to evaluate the Accords as legal and political documents. He concludes that the omission of any provision for the exercise by the Afghan people of their internationally-backed right to self-determination remitted the resolution of the Afghan conflict to the battlefield, at potentially great cost for the civilian population.

The prospects for orderly government in Afghanistan are taken up by Louis Dupree. He outlines in considerable detail the cultural responses which prevented communist rule from taking root in Afghanistan, and draws on these to elucidate questions relating to the repatriation of the external refugee population, and the forms which government in Afghanistan after the Soviet withdrawal may take in the medium-to-long term. He believes that in the long-run, a federated Islamic republic based on substantial regional autonomy provides the best prospect for effective resolution of the Afghan conflict, and that efforts by outside regional powers to determine Afghanistan's political future are likely to be fruitless.

The consequences of Soviet withdrawal for the regional states of Pakistan, Iran, and India are explored in detail by Amin Saikal. He notes that the Soviet invasion of Afghanistan provoked complex adjustments in the regional and global positions of each of these powers, and that these adjustments determine in part the implications for the states of Soviet withdrawal. None the less, these are also partly determined by exactly what happens in Afghanistan in the wake of Soviet withdrawal, and by changes which may consequently take place in the foreign policies of the other regional states. He draws on three broad scenarios of political developments in Afghanistan in order to investigate the more important of these implications.

The consequences for the Soviet Union of its Afghan debacle are discussed by T.H. Rigby. While doubting that the impact of the withdrawal will be deep-going or persistent, he sees substantial economic and political advantages flowing from the Soviet leadership's willingness to cut its losses in Afghanistan, and argues that important theoretical conclusions may be derived from the Afghan experience. Taking a longer perspective, he points to the distinctive attitudes of Soviet veterans of the war (*afgantsy*), and of Muslims in Soviet Central Asia alienated by the prosecution of the war, as factors which may impact seriously on Soviet domestic politics in the future.

Geoffrey Jukes focuses on the lessons which the Soviet armed forces may be disposed to draw from the Afghan experience. He notes that the armed forces are largely prepared for major war against the US and its allies, and that the forces which invaded Afghanistan were ill-equipped to engage in counterinsurgency activities. None the less, because of this very focus on major war, the lessons which could be learned from the war in Afghanistan were necessarily of minor relevance, something reflected in the muted treatment which the war received until 1986 in the military publications *Krasnaia zvezda* and *Kommunist vooruzhennykh sil*. He emphasises that as a consequence of the official policy of *glasnost'* ('publicity'), the Soviet armed forces are now meeting with criticism on a range of grounds, of which the conduct of the Afghan war is but one.

The reactions, to the withdrawal, from Soviet allies in Eastern Europe are investigated by Robert F. Miller. He identifies distinctions which the Soviets have drawn between different categories of alliance partner, and argues that the withdrawal from Afghanistan marks not simply a change in Afghanistan's status, but tacitly a breakdown in the distinct category of states of 'socialist orientation'. He identifies liberal and conservative positions in the reactions of Eastern European states to the withdrawal from Afghanistan, but emphasises that it is premature to conclude from the fact of the withdrawal that the Brezhnev Doctrine is on the point of collapse.

The position of the withdrawal in the complex politics of Sino-Soviet relations is discussed by Leslie Holmes. He makes it clear that the withdrawal alone will not allay Chinese suspicions of Soviet global intentions; and after outlining the emergence of the Sino-Soviet dispute, identifies the different ways in which China was influenced by the Soviet invasion. He notes a number of factors which may impinge upon Sino-Soviet relations *other* than the three which the Chinese have reiterated—Afghanistan, Border Forces, and Kampuchea—and concludes that while relations between the two powers may improve appreciably, this is unlikely in the changed context of the 1980s to pose a threat to the West.

The place of the Afghanistan 'settlement' in the future of world politics is analysed by Richard A. Falk. He regards effective opposition to the Soviet invasion of Afghanistan as one of the few genuine triumphs of the approach to foreign policy of the Reagan Administration. He sees support to the *Mujahideen* as very different from support for the Nicaraguan Contras; the former, in his view, advances the cause of self-determination while the latter inhibits it. He argues that a thoughtful Western response may reinforce those Soviet leaders who favour the withdrawal, and contribute to a solid footing for a new *détente*, and at least a dramatic muting of the Cold War. While the indifference of the Geneva negotiators to the fate of the Afghans during the transition period points to the primacy of geopolitics, the effectiveness of the Afghan resistance illustrates the primacy of politics over mere military strength in world affairs. Noting that the withdrawal of Soviet forces does not add up to the attainment of peace and justice for the Afghan people, he concludes with a powerful plea that they not be abandoned and forgotten by Western governments.

The volume concludes with a chapter by J.L. Richardson, who seeks to identify certain key themes which run through the earlier chapters, and to delineate the characteristics of the Afghan crisis—notably the abundance and decentralised character of actors—which made it peculiarly difficult to manage. In doing so, he notes the contrast between the Afghan case and the earlier precedent of negotiated US disengagement from the war in Vietnam, in the context of more general ideas about the conditions conducive to the effective practice of crisis diplomacy.

FOOTNOTES

1   See Raymond L. Garthoff, *Détente and Confrontation: American-Soviet Relations from Nixon to Reagan* (Washington D.C.: The Brookings Institution, 1985) p.887.

2   Soviet concern became especially marked after a publicly-acknowledged coup attempt against the regime: see BBC *Summary of World Broadcasts* FE/0292/C/5, 26 October 1988. On 13 November 1988, Mikhail Leshchinskii observed on Soviet television that 'the party, as before, is being torn by contradictions between fractions and wings' and that the PDPA 'has no support in the people': BBC *Summary of World Broadcasts* SU/0309/A3/1, 15 November 1988.

3   These processes are discussed from somewhat different perspectives in Vartan Gregorian, *The Emergence of Modern Afghanistan: Politics of Reform and Modernization 1880-1946* (Stanford: Stanford University Press, 1969); Hasan Kawun Kakar, *Government and Society in Afghanistan: The Reign of Amir 'Abd al-Rahman Khan* (Austin: University of Texas Press, 1979); and Michael Barry, *Le Royaume de l'Insolence: La résistance afghane du Grand Moghol à l'invasion soviétique* (Paris: Flammarion, 1984).

4   This involved episode is examined in greater detail in Leon B. Poullada, *Reform and Rebellion in Afghanistan, 1919-1929: King Amanullah's Failure to Modernize a Tribal Society* (Ithaca: Cornell University Press, 1973); and in M. Nazif Shahrani, 'State Building and Social Fragmentation in Afghanistan: A Historical Perspective', in Ali Banuazizi and Myron Weiner (eds.), *The State, Religion, and Ethnic Politics: Afghanistan, Iran, and Pakistan* (Syracuse: Syracuse University Press, 1986) pp.23-74.

5   For a discussion of US diplomacy in this period, see Leon B. Poullada, 'Afghanistan and the United States: The Crucial Years', *The Middle East Journal*, vol.35, no.2, Spring 1981, pp.178-190.

6   Henry S. Bradsher, *Afghanistan and the Soviet Union* (Durham: Duke University Press, 1985) pp.21-28.

7   See Anthony Arnold, *Afghanistan's Two-Party Communism: Parcham and Khalq* (Stanford: Hoover Institution Press, 1983) pp.23-63.

8   On the politics of the 'constitutional period', see Sabahuddin Kushkaki, *Daha-i Qanun Asasi: Ghaflat Zadagi Afghanha wa Fursat Talabi Rusha* (Peshawar: Shurai-i saqafati Jihad-i Afghanistan, 1986).

9   This brought him into open conflict with L.I. Brezhnev during a visit to the Soviet Union in April 1977: see Abdul Samad Ghaus, *The Fall of Afghanistan: An Insider's Account* (McLean: Pergamon-Brassey's, 1988) pp.178-179.

10   On land reform, see Latif Tabibi, 'Die afghanische Landreform von 1979: Ihre Vorgeschichte und Konsequenzen', unpublished Doctoral Dissertation, Freie Universität Berlin, 1981. On the position of women see Nancy Hatch Dupree, 'Revolutionary Rhetoric and Afghan Women', in M. Nazif Shahrani and Robert L. Canfield (eds.), *Revolutions & Rebellions in Afghanistan: Anthropological Perspectives* (Berkeley: Institute of International Studies, University of California, 1986) pp.306-340.

11 The Soviet invasion has received detailed attention in a number of monographs. These include Bradsher, *op.cit.*, pp.96-125; Garthoff, *op.cit.*, pp.895-937; Thomas T. Hammond, *Red Flag Over Afghanistan: The Communist Coup, The Soviet Invasion, and the Consequences* (Boulder: Westview Press, 1984); Anthony Arnold, *Afghanistan: The Soviet Invasion in Perspective* (Stanford: Hoover Institution Press, 1985); and Joseph J. Collins, *The Soviet Invasion of Afghanistan: A Study in the Use of Force in Soviet Foreign Policy* (Lexington: Lexington Books, 1986).

12 The use of terror by the regime and its Soviet backers is by now very well documented. See *Rapport sur la situation des droits de l'homme en Afghanistan* (E/CN.4/1985/21, Human Rights Commission, Economic and Social Council, United Nations, 19 February 1985); *Situation of Human Rights in Afghanistan* (A/40/843, General Assembly, United Nations, 5 November 1985); *Report on the Situation of Human Rights in Afghanistan* (E/CN.4/1986/24, Human Rights Commission, Economic and Social Council, United Nations, 17 February 1986); *Situation of Human Rights in Afghanistan* (A/41/778, General Assembly, United Nations, 9 January 1987); *Report on the Situation of Human Rights in Afghanistan* (A/42/667, General Assembly, United Nations, 23 October 1987); Amnesty International, *Democratic Republic of Afghanistan: Background Briefing on Amnesty International's Concerns* (London: ASA/11/13/83, October 1983); Amnesty International, *Afghanistan: Torture of Political Prisoners* (London: ASA/11/04/86, November 1986); Amnesty International, *Afghanistan—Unlawful Killings and Torture* (London: ASA/11/02/88, May 1988); Bernard Dupaigne (ed.), *Les droits de l'homme en Afghanistan* (Paris: AFRANE, 1985); Michael Barry, Johan Lagerfelt and Marie-Odile Terrenoire, 'International Humanitarian Enquiry Commission on Displaced Persons in Afghanistan', *Central Asian Survey*, vol.5, no.1, 1986, pp.65-99; and outstandingly, Jeri Laber and Barnett R. Rubin, *"A Nation is Dying": Afghanistan under the Soviets 1979-87* (Evanston: Northwestern University Press, 1988).

13 See Amin Saikal, 'Islam: resistance and reassertion', *The World Today*, vol.43, no.11, November 1987, pp.191-194.

14 For a detailed and penetrating analysis of the *Mujahideen*, see Olivier Roy, *Islam and Resistance in Afghanistan* (Cambridge: Cambridge University Press, 1986).

15 On these dilemmas, see Amin Saikal, *The Afghanistan Conflict: Gorbachev's Options* (Canberra: Canberra Papers on Strategy and Defence no.42, Strategic and Defence Studies Centre, Research School of Pacific Studies, Australian National University, 1987) pp.34-49.

2

The Geneva Accords of April 1988

William Maley

At a ceremony in the *Palais des Nations* in Geneva on 14 April 1988, the Government of Pakistan and the Kabul-based regime of the People's Democratic Party of Afghanistan signed a series of Accords dealing with Afghanistan's future. Nearly a decade had passed since non-communist rule had been brought to an end by the violent coup staged by disgruntled supporters of the People's Democratic Party in the Afghan armed forces; and over eight years had elapsed since Soviet forces invaded Afghanistan in December 1979 to replace the erratic President Hafizullah Amin, of the ruling party's *Khalq* faction, with their trusted ally Babrak Karmal, of the *Parcham* faction. Much had happened following the invasion. Karmal, a despised and ineffectual figure, had himself been replaced in May 1986 by his *Parcham* colleague Dr Najibullah, who had headed the regime's secret police (KHAD) from 1980 to 1985.

Yet these petty quarrels were the least of Afghanistan's traumas. The Soviet invasion had met with mass opposition, spearheaded by groups of Islamic resistants (*Mujahideen*) with bases in Pakistan and Iran; and the technology of modern warfare had been turned directly against the Afghan people, millions of whom fled as refugees to neighbouring countries. The costs of the war were horrendous. According to a Soviet spokesman, by mid-1988, 13310 Soviet soldiers had died in Afghanistan,[1] amply justifying General Secretary Gorbachev's February 1986 description of Afghanistan as a 'bleeding wound' (*krovotochashchaia rana*).[2] However, compared to the casualties in the vulnerable Afghan civilian population, this was a trivial figure: a detailed study in 1988 calculated that roughly 9% of the Afghan population, or 1.24 million people, had died as a result of aerial bombing raids, shootings, artillery shellings, antipersonnel mines, exhaustion and other war-related conditions.[3] Afghanistan in some places was so devastated that a British journalist, visiting the once-fertile countryside, remarked that it was as if someone had dropped a bomb in the Garden of Eden.[4]

Many factors apart from the Accords will shape the future of Afghanistan and the Southwest Asian region. None the less, the Accords merit careful scrutiny. To provide such scrutiny is the aim of this chapter. It is divided into five sections. The first examines the organisational context and the distinctive features of the negotiating process. The second highlights the political developments which brought the negotiations to a head. The third outlines the major provisions of the Accords. The fourth contains some brief comments about the accords as strictly *legal* documents. The fifth treats the Accords as *political* documents and provides a preliminary assessment of them from a number of different perspectives.

The Development of the Negotiating Process

The Soviet invasion of Afghanistan was met by firm and immediate international condemnation. In January 1980, pursuant to the *Uniting for Peace* resolution, the United Nations Security Council called an emergency Special Session of the UN General Assembly which overwhelmingly adopted a resolution calling for 'the immediate, unconditional and total withdrawal of the foreign troops from Afghanistan'.[5] None the less, the UN reaction from the beginning was marked by a certain ambivalence. Most strikingly, the General Assembly accepted the credentials of the delegation of the Soviet-installed puppet regime in Kabul which duly voted against the resolution. This was a most unfortunate move, which contrasted sharply with the situation which prevailed between 1956-1963, when the credentials of the delegation of the Hungarian regime of Janos Kádár were not approved.[6] It gave the regime a standing no other puppet regime had been granted since the UN's establishment,[7] and significantly shaped the character of subsequent negotiations over Afghanistan.

More seriously, the West allowed the issues for these negotiations to be determined substantially by the USSR—a classic weakness of Western negotiating style.[8] On 14 May 1980, the Kabul regime issued at Moscow's behest a statement directed at Iran and Pakistan, outlining a program for a 'political solution' to the 'tension that has come about in this region'.[9] Its program was to be precisely mirrored in the agenda of the subsequent negotiations conducted under UN auspices, which dealt with the withdrawal of the foreign troops, non-interference in the internal affairs of states, international guarantees, and the voluntary return of the refugees to their homes. This was a notable victory for the Soviet Union: the issue of self-determination for the Afghan people, also mentioned by the General Assembly, of course did *not* figure in Kabul's program, and its exclusion effectively subordinated the General Assembly's conditions for an acceptable settlement to those specified by the Soviet leadership.

Kabul's proposals met with a frosty response from Pakistan, which was reluctant to take any step which could be interpreted as signifying diplomatic recognition of the Karmal regime. This difficulty was overcome in 1982 when Señor Diego Cordovez, the Personal Representative of the UN Secretary-General, took over the management of communications between Kabul and Islamabad which had been instigated by Javier Pérez de Cuéllar in April 1981. Cordovez inaugurated a series of negotiations in Geneva and acted as go-between in order to overcome Pakistan's objections to direct contacts with representatives of the Kabul regime.[10] The *Mujahideen* were excluded from the negotiations, and in sympathy Iran declined to participate directly. In 1983, following the death in November 1982 of Soviet General Secretary L.I. Brezhnev[11] and his replacement by Iu.V. Andropov, there was a flurry of optimism.[12] It proved to be ill-founded, largely because of the Soviet refusal to allow the nature of the Kabul regime to figure on the agenda of the discussions. However, by June 1985, instruments covering the principles of

14

mutual relations and the voluntary return of refugees were virtually completed, and a declaration of guarantees was forwarded for comment to the USA and the USSR. In December 1985, possibly without the knowledge of President Reagan, the US Administration committed itself to end military aid to the *Mujahideen* at the beginning of a Soviet troop withdrawal.[13] The obstacle to the completion of the settlement package therefore lay in the preconditions and timetable for Soviet withdrawal. In order to understand how this problem was overcome, it is necessary to pay some attention to the *politics* of the negotiations.

The Turning Point

A number of considerations undermined the Soviet leadership's enthusiasm for the war in Afghanistan. Some related to changing conditions in the USSR itself. First, the war in Afghanistan was never popular. An opinion survey published in mid-1985 suggested that only one quarter of the Soviet adult urban population approved of Soviet policy in Afghanistan or expressed 'confidence in the eventual success of official policy'.[14] This finding was reinforced in a number of other studies, which emphasised the particular intensity of opposition in the Central Asian and Baltic republics of the USSR.[15] Second and more importantly, the character of the Soviet leadership itself changed.[16] By early 1988, most of those who had been voting members of the Politburo at the time of the invasion of Afghanistan had either died (L.I. Brezhnev, A.N. Kosygin, M.A. Suslov, Iu.V Andropov, K.U. Chernenko, A.Ia. Pel'she and D.F. Ustinov), or been retired (A.P. Kirilenko, G.V. Romanov, N.A. Tikhonov, V.V. Grishin, and D.A. Kunaev). Only A.A. Gromyko and V.V. Shcherbitskii remained in office. This leadership change prepared the ground—as Jerry F. Hough anticipated in 1980—for 'a more activist and innovative foreign policy'.[17]

Other considerations arose from the dispiriting developments within Afghanistan. First, the Kabul regime was from the beginning rent by irremediable factional strife, which it proved unable to overcome.[18] In early 1987, this was reported on Soviet television when the political commentator Aleksandr Bovin referred to the 'negative role' of the 'dissensions, feuds and

15

bloody clashes within the ruling party itself'.[19] It had no claim to legitimacy, and was therefore forced to rely for its survival on the continued availability of Soviet military protection.[20] Second, the costs of the USSR's military campaign escalated dramatically in the second half of 1986, when the *Mujahideen* obtained US-supplied Stinger anti-aircraft missiles manufactured by General Dynamics. Up to that point, the Soviet Union had been able to meet a substantial proportion of the direct costs of its intervention by exploiting Afghanistan's natural resources.[21] Soviet strategy had placed emphasis on attacking the civilian populations from which the *Mujahideen* drew support, and this led to the deployment of expensive weapons systems such as the MI-24 ('Hind') helicopter gunship, and the MiG-23 ('Flogger') and Su-25 ('Frogfoot') fighter-bombers. To counter these, the resistance until the arrival of the Stinger missiles had only relatively primitive SAM-7 missiles. This imbalance was largely the product of US bureaucratic politics: certain officials in the US Central Intelligence Agency vigorously resisted moves to supply the resistance with more sophisticated anti-aircraft systems,[22] arguing *inter alia* that their supply would simply prompt Soviet escalation. Just how misguided these officials were became clear when the Stinger missiles were ultimately deployed. In terms of equipment the cost of the war for the Soviets rocketed—according to one source, the USSR lost 512 aircraft and helicopters between January and November 1987[23]—and the Soviet response was *not* to escalate, but rather to revive diplomatic moves directed at procuring a settlement of the conflict.

Until 1988, it is fair to say, the Kremlin showed little concern to address in Geneva any of the substantive issues at the heart of the Afghan conflict. Its objective was rather to sustain the negotiating *process*.[24] However, on 8 February 1988, General Secretary Gorbachev signalled a change in the Soviet leadership's approach. He announced a specific date, 15 May 1988, for beginning the withdrawal of Soviet troops, and a ten-month period for the completion of the withdrawal. He based this on the assumption that agreements would be signed no later than 15 March 1988.[25] The statement was extraordinarily shrewd. It created the impression that a unique opportunity could be missed if Islamabad and Washington failed to cooperate. Furthermore, without making any concession to the major concern of the

Mujahideen, namely the right of the Afghan people to self-determination, it appealed blatantly to the USA's desire to secure a Soviet troop withdrawal. This minimised the danger that the self-determination question would be effectively raised.

The Geneva talks resumed at the beginning of March 1988. The Kabul regime's representative offered a nine-month withdrawal period, with half the Soviet contingent to be withdrawn in the first three months.[26] The offer that the withdrawal be 'front-end loaded' went some way towards meeting a major concern expressed by US Secretary of State George Shultz: that in the absence of 'front-end loading', the *Mujahideen* would be exposed (as a result of the Administration's December 1985 commitment) to nine months of fierce attack to which they might lack the weaponry to respond. None the less, this was only one aspect of a broader US concern articulated in particular by Congressional allies of the resistance—that the draft agreements obliged outside supporters of the *Mujahideen* to cease their support, but left the Soviet Union free to supply whatever support it chose to the Kabul regime. On this there was no formal compromise. Shultz proposed to the Soviet Union that US support for the resistance should be allowed for as long as Soviet support for the regime was maintained. A response was received in a letter from Soviet Foreign Minister Shevardnadze. According to Michael Gordon, after 'some debate within the Administration, it was decided that the letter and oral presentations by Soviet diplomats constituted a positive response to the American plan and Mr Shultz recommended accepting the deal'.[27] Once the Administration accepted Shevardnadze's response, the State Department applied intense pressure on the Pakistan Government to abandon its demand for a new Government in Kabul and sign the accords.[28] This pressure Pakistan was unable to withstand.

The Content of the Accords

The First Geneva Accord was entitled *Bilateral Agreement Between the Republic of Afghanistan and the Islamic Republic of Pakistan on the Principles of Mutual Relations, in particular on Non-Interference and Non-Intervention*. It set out thirteen separate obligations undertaken by each High Contracting Party.

Five are especially noteworthy. Article II(4) obliged each party 'to ensure that its territory is not used in any manner which would violate the sovereignty, political independence, territorial integrity and national unity or disrupt the political, economic and social stability of the other High Contracting Party'. Article II(7) imposed the obligation 'to refrain from the promotion, encouragement or support, direct or indirect, of rebellious or secessionist activities against the other High Contracting Party, under any pretext whatsoever, or from any other action which seeks to disrupt the unity or to undermine or subvert the political order of the other High Contracting Party'. The obligation in Article II(8) was 'to prevent within its territory the training, equipping, financing and recruitment of mercenaries from whatever origin for the purpose of hostile activities against the other High Contracting Party, or the sending of such mercenaries into the territory of the other High Contracting Party and accordingly to deny facilities, including financing for the training, equipping and transit of such mercenaries'. Article II(11) required each party 'to prevent any assistance to or use of or tolerance of terrorist groups, saboteurs or subversive agents against the other High Contracting Party.' Most importantly, Article II(12) outlined the obligation 'to prevent within its territory the presence, harbouring, in camps and bases or otherwise, organising, training, financing, equipping and arming of individuals and political, ethnic and any other groups for the purpose of creating subversion, disorder or unrest in the territory of the other High Contracting Party and accordingly also to prevent the use of mass media and the transportation of arms, ammunition and equipment by such individuals and groups'.

The Second Geneva Accord was entitled *Declaration on International Guarantees*, and its signatories were the USSR and the USA. The signatories undertook 'to invariably refrain from any form of interference and intervention in the internal affairs of the Republic of Afghanistan and the Islamic Republic of Pakistan and to respect the commitments contained in the bilateral Agreement between the Republic of Afghanistan and the Islamic Republic of Pakistan on the Principles of Mutual Relations, in particular on Non-Interference and Non-Intervention.'

The Third Geneva Accord was entitled *Bilateral Agreement between the Republic of Afghanistan and the Islamic Republic of Pakistan on the Voluntary Return of Refugees*. It provided that all

Afghan refugees 'temporarily present in the territory of the Islamic Republic of Pakistan shall be given the opportunity to return voluntarily to their homeland in accordance with the arrangements and conditions set out in the present agreement'. Those arrangements and conditions were set out in some detail.

The Fourth Geneva Accord was entitled *Agreement on the Interrelationships for the Settlement of the Situation relating to Afghanistan*. It was signed by the representatives of the Kabul regime and the Government of Pakistan, and in witness, the representatives of the States-Guarantors, the USSR and USA, affixed their signatures. It stated that all Accords would enter into force on 15 May 1988. Its key provision was contained in Paragraph 5: 'In accordance with the timeframe agreed upon between the Union of Soviet Socialist Republics and the Republic of Afghanistan there will be a phased withdrawal of the foreign troops which will start on the date of entry into force mentioned above. One half of the troops will be withdrawn by 15 August 1988 and the withdrawal of all troops will be completed within nine months'. An annexed *Memorandum of Understanding* dealt with the 'modalities and logistical arrangements' for the work of a representative of the Secretary-General, and personnel under his authority, who 'shall investigate any possible violations of any of the provisions of the instruments and prepare a report thereon'.

To coincide with the signing of the Accords, the US Secretary of State transmitted to the Secretary-General an official Statement. The key paragraph read: 'The obligations undertaken by the guarantors are symmetrical. In this regard, the United States has advised the Soviet Union that the U.S. retains the right, consistent with its obligations as guarantor, to provide military assistance to parties in Afghanistan. Should the Soviet Union exercise restraint in providing military assistance to parties in Afghanistan, the U.S. similarly will exercise restraint'.[29]

Legal Aspects of the Accords

The Accords were not simply the outcome of a negotiating process, but legal documents, and as legal documents they raised a number of intriguing issues. These included not simply matters of interpretation, but questions relating to the source of obligations under international law. The following remarks can only touch the surface of problems of considerable complexity.

The two *Bilateral Agreements* plainly fell within the definition of 'treaty' set out in Article 2(1)(a) of the *Vienna Convention on the Law of Treaties*,[30] namely 'an international agreement concluded between States in written form and governed by international law, whether embodied in a single instrument or in two or more related instruments and whatever its particular designation'. As such they were clearly embraced by the principle *pacta sunt servanda*, now codified in Article 26 of the *Vienna Convention* as providing that every 'treaty in force is binding upon the parties to it and must be performed by them in good faith'. However, the status of the *Declaration* was not nearly so clear-cut. Unlike the three *Agreements*, it contained no provision as to which of the equally authentic texts should prevail in the event of any divergence of interpretation. This could be taken to imply that the *Declaration* did not import obligations about the performance of which there could be dispute. Furthermore, the treaty-making power of a US Administration is limited: under Article II(2) of the Constitution of the United States, the President 'shall have Power, by and with the Advice and Consent of the Senate, to make Treaties, provided two-thirds of the Senators present concur.' The same is true in respect of the Soviet Union: Article 121(6) of the 1977 Constitution (Fundamental Law) of the USSR provides that 'The Presidium of the Supreme Soviet of the USSR shall ratify and denounce international treaties of the USSR.' The failure of the *Declaration* to provide that it would become operative only upon ratification therefore could suggest that it was not intended by the United States or the Soviet Union that it constitute a treaty importing the obligations upon states to which treaties give rise.

Even declarations made by way of unilateral acts concerning legal or factual situations may have the effect of creating legal obligations. This was the position taken by the International Court of Justice in the case of *Australia* v. *France*, the criterion in point being whether 'it is the intention of the state making the declaration that it should become bound according to its terms.'[31] In the immediate case, however, it was clear from Secretary Shultz's 14 April *Statement* that the intention of the United States in signing the *Declaration* was limited, and that the *Declaration* was to be read in the light of the content of the *Statement* (and

20

that the Soviet Union had been so advised). Thus, no legal objection could be raised to US military assistance to parties in Afghanistan provided it was supplied *under the circumstances outlined in the Statement.*

The status of the timetable for the withdrawal of 'the foreign troops' from Afghanistan also deserves attention from a legal point of view. There was no provision for the Fourth Geneva Accord to come into effect only upon ratification, which suggests that like the *Declaration*, the Fourth Accord was not intended by the USSR or the USA to give rise to mutual treaty obligations. Any complaint at law about departure from the timetable could lie only against the Kabul regime and not against the Soviet Union directly. Paragraph 8 of the Fourth Accord did report that the Accord had 'been examined by the representatives of the Parties to the bilateral agreements and of the States-Guarantors, who have signified their consent with its provisions.' A direct complaint at law about a departure from the timetable could therefore be based on the argument that the Soviet Union's consent to the Accord's provisions constituted a unilateral declaration of the kind considered in *Australia* v. *France.* However, the signatures of the representatives of the USSR and USA were affixed to the Fourth Accord in 'witness' of the signatures of the representatives of Pakistan and the Kabul regime. In the light of this wording there might be some doubt as to whether the Fourth Accord could be held to bind the Soviet Union even as a unilateral declaration.

Beyond these structural problems, one cannot but be struck by the imprecise *wording* of particular provisions in the Accords. Any such imprecision in a legal document creates endless opportunities for dispute. For example, the Accords contained no definition of 'the foreign troops'. This was a point of some substance, as from 1979 onwards, the USSR had despatched to Afghanistan thousands of advisers to direct the operation of Afghan ministries and units of the Afghan armed forces. Following the signing of the Accords, this matter was raised at a press conference held by Najibullah. He remarked: 'As is known, co-operation between Afghanistan and the USSR in the military sphere began 23 years before the April revolution. It has always played an important role in strengthening the defence capability of our state. We have no intention of renouncing the USSR's help in this sphere, at least as long as the situation on the

21

borders of our homeland obliges us to show concern for the interests of our security.'[32]

The other major area of obscurity arose from the language of the First Accord. Expressions which cried out for definition included 'mercenaries', 'terrorist groups', 'saboteurs', and 'subversive agents'. On the one hand, the Kabul regime and the Soviet Union had always described the popular resistance in Afghanistan as 'outside intervention' by individuals of this type. On the other hand, if one accepts the view, argued recently by W. Michael Reisman, that the Afghan *Mujahideen* have engaged in what under international law is a war of national liberation,[33] one would deny that the combatant *Mujahideen* could at law be characterised by these terms.

The Accords as Political Documents

The loose wording of the Accords may have reflected haste and sloppy thinking on the part of the negotiators. At the same time, it could have been symptomatic of something else: that the Accords were designed primarily as *political* documents performing functions which imprecise wording need not hinder.

When one attempts to assess the Accords as political documents, one may pose questions of three different types. After outlining the general form of these questions, I will attempt to provide some preliminary answers. This is hardly a straightforward task. As so often is the case when one appraises acts of diplomacy, one's conclusions may be heavily influenced by views of the motives of the signatories and the extent to which they can be trusted in the long run to honour at least the spirit if not the letter of agreements. Furthermore, it will be some time yet before dusk falls on the Afghan conflict, and the Owl of Minerva is clinging determinedly to her perch.

First, one might ask whether the agreements were in some sense 'good'. An answer will depend upon the criteria one advances to distinguish good from bad agreements. In general, the time-frame within which one is thinking, one's chosen unit of analysis, and ultimately one's values can all shape one's judgment of the worth of an agreement. Second, in the light of one's chosen criteria one can ask whether the agreements made things 'better' than they would have been had no agreement been signed. This is a peculiarly awkward issue to confront, for it enmeshes one in the realm of counterfactuals: one cannot know with certainty whether things would have been 'better' or not. Third, in the light of given criteria one might ask whether the agreements were in some sense the 'best' that could have been secured. This again raises a counterfactual problem: one cannot know with certainty whether a 'better' set of agreements in some sense might not ultimately have been secured had the Accords not been signed.

The successive resolutions adopted by the United Nations General Assembly do not provide a comprehensive statement of the criteria which mark a 'good' settlement, but at least they supply a starting point. From November 1981 onwards, each General Assembly resolution called not simply for a political settlement, but for a political settlement 'in accordance with the provisions of the present resolution'. These resolutions in turn called for an 'immediate withdrawal of the foreign troops from Afghanistan', and reaffirmed 'the right of the Afghan people to determine their own form of government and to choose their economic, political and social system free from outside intervention, subversion, coercion or constraint of any kind whatsoever.'[34] The resolutions reflected the prohibition, in customary international law and Article 2(4) of the *Charter of the United Nations* of 1945, of 'the threat or use of force against the territorial integrity or political independence of any State'; and also the principle of self-determination of peoples set out in the 1970 General Assembly *Declaration on Principles of International Law concerning Friendly Relations and Co-operation among States in accordance with the Charter of the United Nations.*[35]

A first weakness of the Accords when judged against the demands of the General Assembly was that they fell short of requiring 'immediate' Soviet withdrawal. To allow a nine-month withdrawal period for an invasion force with such an abominable record of human rights violations and atrocities was rather like sanctioning a nine-month winding-down period for Auschwitz. This may be a somewhat harsh criticism: negotiators understandably see their undertaking as the art of the possible, and those who conducted the Geneva negotiations may have felt that they were justified in concluding that a nine-month withdrawal period marked the absolute limit of likely Soviet concessions. At the same time, the absence from the negotiations of any representatives of the Afghan civilian population or *Mujahideen* meant that the objective of truncating the withdrawal in order to protect the civilian population had to compete with a range of other interests which the negotiators were pursuing, and which doubtless appeared to them more pressing. This is an excellent illustration of the way in which the criteria for a 'good' settlement can vary according to whether one's perspective is from 'above' or 'below'. Further, the provision for 'front-end loading' of the withdrawal was patently of limited value. The Soviets always used in combat operations only a minority of their forces in Afghanistan at any given time, and their air capability in particular survived largely intact even as a large number of ground troops were withdrawn.[36]

But the most serious weakness of all was the omission from the Accords of any provision for self-determination. The idea of self-determination is in some ways quite elusive. As R.J. Vincent has argued, there are problems 'of definition of the "self" and of how it is to be "determined".'[37] Yet it is a right which the Soviet Union for its own reasons has championed for many years,[38] and it is hardly now the moment to suggest that it was incapable of realisation through agreements such as those signed in Geneva. In the Afghan context, self-determination is best construed as a process by which the empirically illegitimate regime in Kabul is replaced by one which enjoys generalised normative support. Self-determination is important not simply as an abstract good, but as a key element in war termination. As Randle has noted, a 'political settlement will be inadequate if the peace negotiators have not reached all the issues and leave unresolved some of the disputes that were the basis for the war.'[39] After the Accords were signed in Geneva, Señor Cordovez visited Pakistan to conduct discussions on the future government of Afghanistan, and even claimed to speak for the 'silent majority' of Afghans. However, his task was awesome. Bacon was careful to emphasise that it 'is better dealing with men in appetite, than with those that are where they would be',[40] and once the Accords came into force, they went quite some way towards leaving the Superpowers satiated.

All this suggests that the Accords fell somewhat short of the type of settlement which General Assembly resolutions had suggested should be sought. Yet it is notoriously the case that something that is not particularly 'good' can be better than nothing. The question therefore arises whether the position for the Afghan people would have been better had no Accords been signed. The main defence of the Accords has been that whatever their defects, they did supply a deadline beyond which no foreign troops were to remain in Afghanistan. Those who believe that the USSR was determined in any case to quit Afghanistan are unlikely to find this defence persuasive. Nonetheless, a further defence, that the Accords provided an indispensable veil for ignominious retreat by a major power, cannot be discounted.

However, one can still query whether the Accords were the best obtainable. The Soviet leadership indeed expressed concern at the raising by Pakistan during the last round of talks of the issue of the replacement of Najibullah's regime by an interim government.[41] Yet this was a perfectly reasonable step on Pakistan's part given the character of the General Assembly's pronouncements on Afghanistan, and it came as a surprise to Moscow only because the talks had so long been deadlocked over the issue of a withdrawal timetable that the possibility that self-determination would become an issue was overlooked. Given the apparent preference of the Soviet Union for some kind of agreement to clothe its retreat in a degree of honour, it seems unlikely that an historic opportunity would have been missed had Pakistan stood firm on this point.

The failure of the Geneva Accords to address the issue of self-determination for the Afghan people constituted their fundamental flaw. The United States and Pakistan negotiated the Geneva Accords in a spirit of hope, and this should not be held against them. Without some hope, it would be pointless ever to resort to negotiation. Yet the ancients warned that hope is by nature an expensive commodity.[42] By avoiding provision for self-determination, the Accords simply remitted the Afghan conflict to the battlefield—possibly making little difference to Afghanistan's long-term political future, but imposing immense short-run costs on the Afghan people. The continuation of ferocious military exchanges well after the Accords came into force grimly confirmed what was obvious from the day the Accords were published—that for many Afghans, they offered only the peace of the grave.

FOOTNOTES

1 'Strogo sobliudat' obiazatel'stva', *Pravda*, 26 May 1988, p.5.

2 *Materialy XXVII s" ezda Kommunisticheskoi partii Sovetskogo Soiuza* (Moscow: Politizdat, 1986) p.69.

3 Marek Sliwinski, *Evaluation des consequences humaines, sociales et écologiques de la guerre en Afghanistan* (Paris: Bureau International Afghanistan and Médecins sans Frontières, 1988) p.5.

4 Gavin Bell, 'Paradise lost in Afghan valley of death', *The Times*, 21 July 1987, p.7.

5 United Nations General Assembly, *Resolution ES-6/2*, 14 January 1980.

6 James Crawford, *The Creation of States in International Law* (Oxford: Oxford University Press, 1979) p.58.

7 See Alan James, *Sovereign Statehood: The Basis of International Society* (London: Allen & Unwin, 1986) pp.140-142. It is interesting to note that James does not classify Kádár's regime in Hungary between 1956-1963 as a 'puppet regime'—which makes the acceptance of the Karmal regime's credentials even more extraordinary.

8 See Fred C. Iklé, *How Nations Negotiate* (New York: Harper & Row, 1964) pp.238-241.

9 For a text of the statement, see BBC *Summary of World Broadcasts* FE/6421/C/1-3, 16 May 1980. The Soviet involvement in its release is obvious. Three hours after it went to air in Pushto on the Kabul Home Service, an English text with additions was issued by TASS.

10 From August 1984, these communications took the form of 'proximity talks'. Delegations from the two capitals occupied separate rooms in the *Palais des Nations* in Geneva, and Cordovez shuttled between the two.

11 During the 26th Congress of the Communist Party of the Soviet Union in February 1981, Brezhnev had adopted an uncompromising position on the role of the Soviet contingent in Afghanistan: '... we will be ready to withdraw it with the agreement of the Afghan government. For this, the infiltration of counter-revolutionary bands into Afghanistan must be completely stopped. This must be secured in understandings between Afghanistan and its neighbours. Reliable guarantees are needed that there will be no new intervention. Such is the fundamental position of the Soviet Union, and we will keep to it firmly.': *XXVI s" ezd Kommunisticheskoi partii Sovetskogo Soiuza: stenograficheskii otchet* (Moscow: Politizdat, 1981) vol.I, p.30.

12 Selig S. Harrison, 'A Breakthrough in Afghanistan?', *Foreign Policy*, no.51, Summer 1983, pp.3-26.

13 David K. Shipler, 'Reagan Didn't Know of Afghan Deal', *The New York Times*, 11 February 1988, p.3.

14 *The Soviet Public and the War in Afghanistan: Perceptions, Prognoses, Information Sources* (Munich: Radio Free Europe/Radio Liberty, Soviet Area Audience and Opinion Research, AR 4-85, June 1985) p.1.

15 See Alexandre Bennigsen, 'The Impact of the Afghan War on Soviet Central Asia', in Rosanne Klass (ed.), *Afghanistan—The Great Game Revisited* (New York: Freedom House, 1987) pp.287-299; Taras Kuzio,

'Opposition in the USSR to the Occupation of Afghanistan', *Central Asian Survey*, vol.6, no.1, 1987, pp.99-117; and Maya Latynski and S. Enders Wimbush, 'The Mujahideen and the Russian Empire', *The National Interest*, no.11, Spring 1988, pp.30-42.

16 See J.H. Miller, 'How Much of a New Elite?', in R.F. Miller, J.H. Miller and T.H. Rigby (eds.), *Gorbachev at the Helm: A New Era in Soviet Politics?* (London: Croom Helm, 1987) pp.61-89.

17 Jerry F. Hough, *Soviet Leadership in Transition* (Washington: The Brookings Institution, 1980) p.166.

18 A failure to give proper weight to the implications of the regime's weakness seriously skews Selig S. Harrison, 'Inside the Afghan Talks', *Foreign Policy*, no.72, Fall 1988, pp.31-60. Harrison has long propounded an idiosyncratic view of the capacities of the Kabul regime. In a remarkable essay, 'The Soviets Are Winning in Afghanistan', *The Washington Post*, 13 May 1984, pp.C1, C4, he admitted that he had 'only a rudimentary knowledge of Afghan languages' and found it necessary during his eight-day visit to Kabul 'to work through a Foreign Ministry interpreter in officially arranged interviews'. None the less, he depicted Kabul as 'a cohesive city-state run by a reasonably unified Afghan communist machine.' Harrison's argument was heavily criticised by specialists: see David C. Champagne and Thomas E. Gouttierre, 'The Russians Are Not Winning in Afghanistan', *The Washington Post*, 26 May 1984, p.A19. In 'Inside the Afghan Talks', he does not repeat his earlier exaggerations; but nor does he repudiate them—and as a result, he overrates the contribution of Cordovez's diplomatic activities in prompting Soviet concessions.

19 BBC *Summary of World Broadcasts* SU/8494/A3/3, 17 February 1987.

20 William Maley, 'Political Legitimation in Contemporary Afghanistan', *Asian Survey*, vol.27, no.6, June 1987, pp.705-725.

21 See John F. Shroder, Jnr. and Abdul Tawab Assifi, 'Afghan Resources and Soviet Exploitation', in Rosanne Klass (ed.), *Afghanistan—The Great Game Revisited* (New York: Freedom House, 1987) pp.97-134, at p.113.

22 John Walcott and Tim Carrington, 'CIA Resisted Proposal To Give Afghan Rebels U.S. Stinger Missiles', *The Wall Street Journal*, 16 February 1988, p.1.

23 A.A. Khan, 'Soviet Strategy in Afghanistan: Success or Failure?', *Defence Journal*, vol.14, nos.1-2, 1988, pp.6-37, at p.30.

24 See Amin Saikal, 'The Afghanistan crisis: a negotiated settlement?', *The World Today*, vol.40, no.11, November 1984, pp.481-489.

25 'Zaiavlenie General'nogo sekretaria TsK KPSS M.S. Gorbacheva po Afganistanu', *Komsomol'skaia pravda*, 9 February 1988, p.1.

26 Paul Lewis, 'New Kabul Offer in Afghan Parley', *The New York Times*, 4 March 1988, p.11.

27 Michael R. Gordon, 'U.S. and Moscow Agree on Pullout from Afghanistan', *The New York Times*, 12 April 1988, p.1.

28 Rosanne Klass, 'Afghanistan: The Accords', *Foreign Affairs*, vol.66, no.5, Summer 1988, pp.922-945, at p.936.

29 *Department of State Bulletin*, vol.88, no.2135, June 1988, p.55. The statement also provided that by 'acting as guarantor of the settlement, the

United States does not intend to imply in any respect recognition of the present regime in Kabul as the lawful government of Afghanistan.' Similarly, on 13 May 1988, the Prime Minister of Pakistan, Mohammad Khan Junejo, stated that 'we have not recognised the present Kabul administration, nor will it be recognised': BBC *Summary of World Broadcasts* FE/0127/C/7, 16 April 1988. These statements were necessary because recognition of the Kabul regime might otherwise have been implied from the signing of the Accords: see Lord McNair, *The Law of Treaties* (London: Oxford University Press, 1961) p.746.

30 For the text of the Convention, see Ian Brownlie (ed.), *Basic Documents in International Law* (Oxford: Oxford University Press, 1983) pp.349-386.

31 I.C.J. Rep. 1974, p.267.

32 BBC *Summary of World Broadcasts* FE/0141/C/1, 3 May 1988.

33 W. Michael Reisman, 'The Resistance in Afghanistan Is Engaged in a War of National Liberation', *American Journal of International Law*, vol.81, no.4, October 1987, pp.906-909. See also Abdul Hakim Tabibi, *The Legal Status of the Afghan Resistance Movement* (Cedar Rapids: Igram Press, 1986).

34 United Nations General Assembly, *Resolutions* 36/34, 18 November 1981; 37/37, 29 November 1982; 38/29, 23 November 1983; 39/13, 15 November 1984; 40/12, 13 November 1985; 41/33, 5 November 1986; 42/15, 10 November 1987.

35 For the texts of the *Charter* and the *Declaration*, see Brownlie (ed.), *op.cit.*, pp.1-44.

36 See Elaine Sciolino, 'U.S. Says Soviets Have Deployed New Attack Jets in Afghanistan', *The New York Times*, 29 October 1988, p.1; and David B. Ottaway, 'U.S. Concerned About Soviets' Use of Bombers in Afghanistan', *The Washington Post*, 1 November 1988, p.27.

37 R.J. Vincent, *Nonintervention and International Order* (Princeton: Princeton University Press, 1974) p.380.

38 Vendulka Kubálková and Albert Cruickshank, *Marxism and International Relations* (Oxford: Oxford University Press, 1985) p.183.

39 Robert F. Randle, *The Origins of Peace: A Study of Peacemaking and the Structure of Peace Settlements* (New York: The Free Press, 1973) p.487.

40 Sir Francis Bacon, 'Of Negotiating', in *Bacon's Essays* (New York: Carlton House, n.d.) pp.259-261, at p.260.

41 Gary Lee, 'Soviets Upset By Terms for Afghan Pact', *The Washington Post*, 15 March 1988, p.1.

42 Thucydides, *History of the Peloponnesian War* (Harmondsworth: Penguin, 1972) p.404.

3

Post-Withdrawal Afghanistan: Light at the End of the Tunnel

Louis Dupree

With the Soviet troop withdrawal, we see the end of Afghanistan's major experience with European imperialism. Most of Africa and Asia were under European imperialist control for at least a hundred years—sometimes longer—but Afghanistan's experience was compressed into less than a decade in the late 20th century. Even then, the Soviets were able to exercise control over only a small portion of the total landscape.

This simply continues the patterns which evolved after the end of World War II. Any colony desiring freedom and supported by the population involved has gained independence. Even the Malaysian Insurgency is no exception, for although General Templer was able to defeat the insurgents, they were mainly *Chinese* Malays, who did not have the support of the non-Chinese peoples. After the suppression of the Communist insurgency, the Malays *did* gain independence from Britain. And the Afghan *Mujahideen*, with the overwhelming assistance of the population, succeeded in convincing the Soviets to leave their country. Never mind that the Soviets insisted they had fulfilled their 'internationalist duty', and that the Afghan army could take care of itself, and that the Republic of Afghanistan (led by the People's Democratic Party of Afghanistan—PDPA) could survive in some form, for all these premises fall down when analysed. By July 1988, even Soviet General K.M. Tsagolov, a former senior military officer in Afghanistan, publicly doubted the survivability of the Kabul regime.[1] But how did this come about? What Afghan patterns helped determine the outcome of the war? Two factors must be briefly discussed: the internal Afghan cultural responses to the war; and the external assistance, which sustained the resistance, and, with the introduction of Stinger and Blowpipe missiles in 1986, turned the tactical war around.

Afghan Cultural Responses[2]

In 1980, when I first began to write about the Soviet invasion, I discussed the patterns which began with the leftist coup of 27-28 April 1978, using seven Rs: Revolution, rhetoric, repression, reforms, revolts, refugees and Russians. I added three more Rs in 1986, the year of the Stingers: Revenge, retribution and Reagan. Now I hope we can conclude with: Retreat, repatriation and reconstruction.

Afghan culture sprang into action (or inaction) as dust from the coup settled over the streets of Kabul and the bodies and disabled tanks were buried or towed away. All the following factors will play major roles as the post-withdrawal patterns emerge.

1. *Can't farm and fight.* The leaders of the new Democratic Republic of Afghanistan (DRA) were pleased that the countryside remained quiet during the first few months after the coup. They did not understand the *seasonal aspects of tribal warfare:* people cannot farm and fight at the same time, as General George Washington found out during the American War for Independence. Many in his militia melted away when the agricultural season began. From spring to autumn, Afghan farmers and herdsmen find themselves engaged in maximum economic activities. In areas where feuds are common, early autumn is the time to begin, for farming and herding cycles give way to times of leisure. And the seasonal feud in Afghanistan permits the Afghan to externalise his internal aggressions—that

is, instead of fighting with his brothers, cousins or other kin, he fights other groups.

2. *Revolts express an opinion.* The regional revolts began right on schedule. The Nuristani in the north-east of Afghanistan went out first, to be ultimately followed by groups in all 29 provinces. In the traditional cultures of the Central Asian-Iranian Plateau areas, first revolts are *not* necessarily designed to *overthrow* but to express *disapproval* of the actions of the central government. In the same tradition, the DRA should have responded with just enough force to stop the revolts and should then have called a *Loya Jirgah* (the traditional Afghan Grand Tribal Assembly) to consider the grievances of the people.

3. *The DRA response.* However, the DRA, with all its new military hardware from the Soviets, overreacted and bombed the regions which revolted, thereby creating a *badal* (blood feud) between the government and the people, so that when spring blossomed in 1979, many of the *Mujahideen* stayed in the field to fight, while others returned to their villages to farm. This was a new cultural signal to the DRA: 'we are now out to overthrow you'. And, in all probability, they would have succeeded if the Soviets had not intervened in December 1979.

4. *Response to the Soviet intervention.* The war became regional in orientation. Tribes and ethnic groups came together whenever DRA and/or Soviet troops intruded into their locality. In Afghanistan, *vertical,* segmentary kin-tribal structures which are found throughout the countryside (with varying degrees of local intensity) band together whenever threatened by an *outside horizontal* force, even though neighbours may be blood enemies. Local enmities are set aside to fight the outsiders. This happened in 1979. This was accentuated by the fact that the ideal male personality type in Afghan society is (again, with varying degrees of intensity) the *warrior-poet*, a man who is brave in battle and articulates well at the village council.

5. *The Islamic factor.* The role of Islam in Afghanistan cannot be over-emphasised. Islam is the umbrella under which all Afghan *Mujahideen* can fight a *jihad* (best translated as 'struggle', *not* 'holy war'). The terms 'moderate' and 'fundamentalist' are often used to describe the seven Pakistan-based political parties described in Chapter One. Yet these are oversimplifications. Only a few 'conservative' (a better term) Afghans want to go back to an idealised Golden Age of Islam,

which never existed except in the minds of a few romantics. Virtually all leaders want to use Islam as a weapon to move Afghanistan into the 21st century—or more accurately, toward the 16th century of Islam.

Although the symbolic manifestations of the new political resurgence in the Islamic world may jar some Western ethnocentric sensitivities, it must be remembered that these symbols are meaningful within their cultural contexts. These include the fashionable anti-Americanism which has infected the Third World, especially among the *literati* and intellectuals. In reality, the Islamic world is trying to re-identify itself in the modern world, because political evolution was stopped—or stymied—by the European imperialists, and when the imperialists gave up political control in the post-World War II period, the newly-independent nations were left with an imperialist-oriented administrative system, geared to the maintenance of law-and-order and the collection of revenue. Now, the former colonies are seeking ways to develop, both economically and politically within their own patterns.

6. *The Commanders evolve.* The pre-war rural power elites in Afghanistan consisted of *collective leadership,* not a single village chief. Westerners usually seek out the leader in a power situation, but in Afghanistan, the leader seldom exists. Naturally, from time to time, one *rish-i-safid* (Persian) or *spin geray* (Pushto, both refer to 'white beards') in a village *jirgah* (often called *majlis* in north Afghanistan) can become dominant, but this is not the ideal, nor usually the reality. The village council usually consists of the heads of lineages (or some such kin-unit) and each is a specialist: water rights, marital problems, property rights, the war chief (who leads in the feuds), and one individual who is the 'go-between' with the nearest government offices. Often, outsiders identify this individual as *the* malik (or khan, beg, and so on—different names in different regions). The 'go-between' would never make a spot decision on an important issue, but would refer the matter to the village council for a collective consensus.

In addition to the *traditional leadership*, two other types of maliks have evolved because of the war inside and outside. The *military commanders* inside have achieved lasting importance and will be integrated into whatever power patterns exist after the Soviet withdrawal. The war accelerated a process which had already begun in the 1960s, after a fair system of conscription was introduced. *Jalbis* (draftees) served for two years in either the army, air force, police, gendarmes, or labour corps, and then most returned to their home villages. Like veterans everywhere, they frequently banded together to compare their common experiences which had occurred *outside* the normal village cultural patterns. These informal rural groups were evolving into local *de facto* (if not *de jure*) power groups before the war. Seldom did they openly challenge the traditional 'white beards', but they made their collective input felt in the decision-making processes. Many of these younger men (now more mature) have become commanders and sub-commanders because of their previous military experience and their charisma. Some are also members of families represented in the traditional village councils. Others are local religious leaders, but no matter what their prior role and status, the military commanders will definitely become a part of the post-war *de jure* power elite.

The second type of new malik is sometimes called the *rupiyah malik* by the Afghan refugees. He is the man who has returned from the Persian Gulf, Saudi Arabia or elsewhere with a small fortune and extensive experience in dealing with outsiders. He often becomes the 'go-between' for the refugees with the Pakistani officials, the United Nations and volunteer agency administrators. Whether or not he can retain a role in the post-withdrawal power elite will depend on his personal and financial contacts (and loans) he has made, and his own charisma. Probably, most will lose their status and role, which had functioned in an unnatural cultural pattern, that is, the refugee situation.

7. *The role of the Seven-Party Alliance.* In May 1985, the seven major political parties in Peshawar were forced into a shot-gun marriage by Pakistan, and other interested parties such as the USA and Saudi Arabia, as well as many inside commanders who insisted that if they (the commanders) could organise cooperative military operations inside Afghanistan, the least the parties could do would be to present a common front to the outside world. Although shaky, the *Islamic Unity of Afghan Mujahideen* held together. The parties performed two valuable functions following the Soviet invasion: they were a major face to the outside world; and also the main avenue of supplies to the resistance.

However, of the seven leaders, only Yunis Khalis (of the *Hezb-i Islami*) could claim a traditional, *territorial* base of power, among the Khugiani Pushtun of the Surkhab region near Jalalabad. The rest, supported by major outside resources (including the USA, Pakistan, and Saudi Arabia), derived their support from *followers*, and followers have the habit of following anyone with the goodies. This does not mean that the six have no roles to perform in the post-withdrawal period, but they will probably have to accommodate themselves to the commanders and the traditional leadership inside, rather than vice-versa. One major fault with the *Islamic Unity of Afghan Mujahideen* as it is constituted is that it includes none of the Shi'ite groups. Other minority groups, such as the Aimaq, Nuristani, and Baluch also lack adequate representation.

8. *Re-migration from the north.* Abdur Rahman Khan (Amir of Afghanistan, 1880-1901) engaged in what I have called 'internal imperialism'.[3] He spread his influence (if not actual control) throughout much of Afghanistan while the Tsarist Russians and the British drew his external boundaries. The amir first subdued dissident elements within his own Durrani Pushtun tribe, and then turned his attention to the other large Pushtun tribe, the Ghilzai, traditional enemies of the Durrani. After this, he moved militarily into the non-Pushtun areas, such as the Hazarajat, Kafiristan and the khanates of northern Afghanistan. Abdur Rahman shifted sizeable numbers of Pushtun to the non-Pushtun areas, making land grants to the Pushtun at the expense of the non-Pushtun.[4] By moving dissident Pushtun elements to live among non-Pushtun peoples of central and north Afghanistan the amir gained two objectives: he removed dissidents from areas where they might continue to create trouble; and he created allies in the non-Pushtun areas, for although the Ghilzai and other Pushtun might be enemies of the Durrani Abdur Rahman in their *own* tribal homelands, they would be pro-Pushtun and supportive of the amir in non-Pushtun territories. In addition, those Pushtun sent to north Afghanistan would serve as 'Guardians of the Marches' up against the Tsarist Central Asian frontier. Some Pushtun went north voluntarily after being given land grants by Abdur Rahman.

The 1979 Soviet invasion of Afghanistan triggered off a pattern that I call 're-migration'. Many of the grandchildren and great-grandchildren of those Pushtun sent to the north by Abdur

Rahman returned to the homes of their ancestors in southern and southwestern Afghanistan. Those re-migrating generally brought their families to refugee camps in Pakistan, and returned to their ancestral homes to fight with *Mujahideen*, who were often distant kinsmen. (It must be added that the non-Pushtun peoples of the north actively 'encouraged' the Pushtun to leave.) Possibly some Pushtun who migrated north to the Kunduz area in the 1930s may return to the north, but they will constitute a minority. The re-migration will be an important factor in post-withdrawal Afghanistan, to be discussed later.

9. *Limited trans-border migration*. Most of the southern border villages and valleys of Afghanistan have been devastated, with their occupants fleeing to Pakistan. In spite of the fact that a favourite Soviet tactic was to use various types of firebombs to burn crops in the fields, some hardy Afghan farmers seasonally crossed the border to plant certain crops, both cereals and vegetables, and periodically returned to try to reap the fruits of their labour. From 1986, when the Stinger and Blowpipe missiles made the air uncomfortable for Soviet pilots, there was an increase in productivity in some regions.[5]

10. *Incipient nationalism*. A subtle linguistic change occurred following the Soviet intervention. During the first few years of the war, the *regional* leaders would speak of 'driving the Soviet and puppet troops from our valley' or 'our region', but many came to speak of 'driving the Soviet invaders out of *Afghanistan*[6], a recognition that *all* the nation was involved in the military actions. This was reinforced by experience in the refugee camps. Despite the numerical predominance of Pushtuns, large pockets of Nuristani, Tajik, Uzbek, Turkman, Hazara, Farsiwan, Badakhshi, and others moved into Refugee Tented Villages. Few camps have had only one ethnic group. The myriad groups have found out they can tolerate—if not love—one another. But the regional ethno-linguistic ties are still the strongest emotions, except among some of the urbanised, Western orientated, and Western-reacting minority.

Will the Refugees Return Home?

This is a question which plagues all concerned: Pakistan and Iran; the United Nations High Commissioner for Refugees

(UNHCR) and other UN agencies, bilateral donors, such as the USA, United Kingdom, France, and West Germany; voluntary agencies (called Non-Government Organisations), and, of course, the refugees themselves. Four major categories of external refugees can be identified:

1. *Those in refugee camps in Pakistan (around 3.5 million) and Iran (around 2 million).* These are primarily from rural areas, and in all probability well over 90% will return to their home villages. This runs counter to the 'mythology' of the refugees as expounded by several groups in Pakistan and echoed by some Westerners. The theory they advance is that the Afghans in refugee camps 'have never had it so good', and do not want to return. Such reasoning ignores the basic fact that three-quarters of the residents in refugee camps are women, children and old people. The bulk of the adult males are inside Afghanistan or have gone elsewhere to work. Legally, the refugees cannot own land in Pakistan, *and* the women do not have the freedom of movement they had in their home villages. Nor can the women contribute to the family's social and economic welfare while living cooped-up in camps. For these reasons, the overwhelming majority of the rurally-oriented refugees want to return home to resume productive lives. And the women wish to return *with* the men for the same reasons. They have suffered psycho-cultural damage more than any other group.[7]

2. *Shopkeepers and entrepreneurs.* Many in the urban category brought capital to Pakistan and either alone or with Pakistani partners entered the business community. Some may remain in Pakistan, but most will probably return to the towns and cities from which they fled. However, I predict that a majority will leave their investments behind in Pakistan, so that they have an economic foot in both countries, thus enhancing the dual economies.

3. *Professionals, intellectuals, technocrats.* In Pakistan, Iran, India and the Gulf States and other Asian nations there have also been *Mujahideen*, although they have collected money and wielded pens instead of weapons. Many of these individuals want to return home. Some, however, have settled their families in Western Europe or North America and will be torn by two forces in the post-withdrawal period: family pressures to stay in the West; patriotic loyalty to help reconstruct Afghanistan. Complicating the situation have been assassinations by the

PDPA regime's secret police of several leading Afghan intellectuals in Pakistan over the past few years. Paradoxically, these hardened the resolve of refugee professionals to remain in Pakistan. A number who had been planning to emigrate to the West postponed their departure.

4. *Professionals, intellectuals, technocrats educated in Western Europe, North America and some educated in the USSR and Eastern Europe, and now living in Europe or North America with their families.* Of these, few will return. Many have been out of Afghanistan for ten years, with children growing up or being born in exile. Whole families have been integrated into Western societies. However, some teachers, doctors, engineers, agricultural specialists and the like, have indicated that they will sign one, two or three year contracts to help their devastated country through its reconstruction period.

A special category of the refugees are the disabled, those wounded badly and with missing limbs, including both sexes of all ages. Little has been done for their rehabilitation in the refugee camps, but in most cases their minds are active and they have some motor ability. Untold thousands exist, and they should be integrated into a free Afghanistan as useful citizens.

The 1.2 million *internal refugees* are another important category. These are the people driven out of their home villages by the war, who settled temporarily either in neighbouring rural areas untouched by the war or around the major towns and cities. The population of Kabul, for example, has swollen from a 1978 population of about 600000 to about 2 million. Some have predicted the internal refugees around cities will be inclined to stay where they are. I disagree, because in the wake of the Soviet withdrawal, there will be little work for internal refugees in the cities, as war-related jobs wither away. Some may integrate into the urban scenes, but the majority will return from where they came; the call of the land is still deeply imprinted in the psyche of the peasant-farmer Afghan, regardless of his or her ethnic identity.

However, one troublesome pattern existed in the Afghan agricultural sector even before 1978: widespread growth of opium poppies in the south and southeast of Afghanistan. Poppy cultivation has now become widespread in the adjacent tribal areas of Pakistan. Returning Afghan refugees will probably continue the growth of this lucrative crop.

The Return of the External Refugees

Whatever the long-term developments in Afghanistan, two facts stand out clearly. First, Afghanistan will never be the same as it was before the 1978 coup. The population has suffered significant losses, and there may be a shortage of farm labour. Table I at page 48 gives the comparative estimated population data for 1978 and 1988. Second, when the refugees return home, they will be once again refugees, but this time in their own land. However, they will not return until the war is over, and not just the Soviet war but the war in general. Estimates vary concerning the rate of refugee return, but the following percentages represent a reasonable consensus: 25-30% within 6 months of the end of the war; another 50% within 7-18 months; another 15-20% after 10 months; 5% will not return. Refugee movements will not occur at a steady rate. The UNHCR has envisaged a possible 'reverse flow', of refugees returning to Pakistan. Several factors could cause this movement: a long civil war, or famine threatened by drought or floods or both.

Those responsible for the return of the refugees have not been idle, and, although none of the many schemes have hardened, discussions and consultations continue unabated. The elaborate plans being drawn up by various organisations will have to be flexible, however, because, as has been said many times, the only thing predictable about the Afghans is their unpredictability. To maximise the efforts of the various agencies of the United Nations (UNHCR, UNICEF, FAO, WFP, WHO, ILO, UNESCO) the Secretary-General Javier Pérez de Cuéllar on 11 May 1988 appointed a former UN High Commissioner for Refugees, Prince Sadruddin Aga Khan, as overall coordinator. The United Nations on 10 June 1988 issued an appeal to all member nations indicating it would be unwise to wait until the war ended to plan for repatriation and reconstruction. In what some saw as undue haste, plans were devised complete with estimated costs. The first phase would be for 18 months (date of commencement unstated), at a cost of $1.16. billion (see Table II at page 49). The figure has been criticised by many, even within the UN structure itself. They ask: Is the figure what is actually necessary, or what the UN can *absorb?* For example, a UNESCO official with no knowledge of Afghanistan flew from Paris to Geneva and spent less than a day discussing possible needs. The writing of the proposal was left to an expert, but the coordinators arbitrarily added an extra zero to his proposed budget.[8] The UNHCR has also projected a four-year period of reconstruction beyond the first 18 months and current estimates set the cost at $839.6 million (Table III at page 50). The assumption is that by the end of the four-year period (1989-93), Afghanistan will be reconstructed and the Afghans well on their way to recovery

Timing of the repatriation will be important. Unfortunately some documents issued by the UN and Non-Government Organisations state that 'spring is the best time to plant in Afghanistan'.[9] However, this is simply not true, for wheat, the basic crop, is planted in early autumn everywhere but in the highland areas of Bamiyan, Ghazni, Ghor and Uruzgan, which do plant a high altitude variety in the spring. Corn and rice can be planted in the spring.

Many refugees will return home under their own devices, but the UN plans to make vehicles available for those who travel along main roads, at least part of the way. In order to help the refugees resume normal lives as quickly as possible, stockpiles of necessary items will be strategically placed along routes of return. Items planned for the stockpiles include: food (or preferably money to purchase food locally in order not to upset the local economy), tents (temporary shelter), medical supplies, seeds, basic agricultural tools, quilts, plastic buckets and portable stoves. Arguments still rage (literally) as to where the stockpiles should be established: on the Pakistan side of the border, or the Afghan side. Critics of the Afghan gambit are convinced that stockpiles on the Afghan side will create a 'pull' factor and maybe encourage the refugees to return too soon. Also, they fear the local commanders will control distribution and favour their followers at the expense of the refugees. Those who criticise the Pakistan stockpile scheme believe a 'push' factor will develop as the Pakistanis virtually force the refugees out, encouraging them to pick up the goodies and go. Credit facilities are being considered, so as not to encourage a 'dependency syndrome'. However, in many parts of Afghanistan loans are never repaid, but guarantee an individual's support to the grantor of the loan.

In order to plan for the reconstruction of the agricultural sector, two maps are needed: (a) a map of all known mine fields;

and (b) a map representing the major areas of agriculture. Map overlays should be prepared to indicate *zones of destruction,* which will aid in planning agricultural reconstruction. Even if the majority of mines are removed, they will remain a menace for years to come. The international community should put pressure on the USSR to remove its mine fields—after all, it planted them—or at the very least demand maps of the fields. The *Mujahideen* commanders could fill in many of the gaps. Plans are underway to acquaint the refugees in the camps with mines, and hopefully to train individuals from most areas how to remove and defuse the mines. This is necessary because several refugees who returned in 1988 to Barikot, an outpost deserted by the Afghan army and their Soviet advisers, lost legs as they wandered into a minefield.

A second map would indicate technological, ecological, agricultural zones in Afghanistan. There are four: (a) in *lalmi* highland, unirrigated cereal-grain fields in the low mountains and foothills, crop-growing is made possible by the rich loess mantle and melt-water run-off; (b) *terraced fields* up hilly slopes have exhibited excellent engineering skills, but water is still lost in downhill flows, and terracing techniques could be improved with technological input; (c) *abi,* open canal irrigation of wheat, rice, maize, vegetable arid fruit gardens can benefit from technological improvements; (d) underground canals called *karez* (Pushto) and *canat* (Persian) bring water to the surface before the water naturally flows to the surface, and diffing and cleaning these well-and-tunnel complexes could be greatly improved with machine technology.

The refugees, as they return to Afghanistan should be *followed* by the technicians capable of helping not only in agricultural reconstruction, but road building, public health, education and the like. In the 350-plus camps in Pakistan, many rural Afghans have been exposed to public health facilities and educational opportunities for the first time in their lives. Few refugee clinics or schools have functioned at full capacity, doctors and nurses have been absent from their posts, medicines have been lost or stolen, teachers, students and textbooks are often absent. But, the important thing is that institutionalisation has begun and should not be permitted to die out. In addition, virtually all the camps in Pakistan have had young Afghans trained as teachers, paramedics, basic engineers, and so on, and *they* should be the ones to follow the refugees home, being paid by the UNHCR, the bilateral programs or the Non-Government Organisations which have trained and paid them for their work in the camps. As mentioned previously, Afghan technocrats who have settled their families in Europe or North American should be given contracts to return and help Afghanistan through its crucial transitional period. And naturally, those who remained in rural Afghanistan and supported the resistance should be embraced in the new developmental networks. For the first time, therefore, those interested in development can begin at the grass roots level and not depend on an inefficient, uninterested, imperialist-oriented centralised bureaucracy haphazardly trying to introduce change from *above*. In post-withdrawal Afghanistan, the process of development can begin at the bottom and evolve to the top.

Some observers have expressed concern over the effects of the PDPA land reforms. On the whole the reforms were a howling failure.[10] Surviving—and I emphasise surviving—land owners will return to original lands, whether devastated, affected by land reform or still tilled by family, friends or tenants. Of course, some disputes will naturally arise, many of which will pre-date the war, but on the whole the return to the land will be peaceful, in the agricultural and economic sense. The political will be something else, as we shall shortly see.

The Political Arena

The repatriation and economic reconstruction may appear difficult, but the political arena defies the most astute appraisals. A number of political developments are possible in post-withdrawal Afghanistan. I shall only consider a few seriously, but most can be rejected immediately, even though they have their partisan supporters, among both Afghans and their sympathisers.

The ideal would be the following: after the fall of the PDPA, a short, bloody transitional period follows, leading to an Islamic Federated Republic, based on autonomous regional units. Some have suggested that Afghanistan could become a second Lebanon, or at least Kabul could become a second Beirut. I do not believe it, because the situation is quite different. Lebanon sits with its back to the mountains and its face to the sea.

41

Afghanistan is landlocked and its land mass is many times that of Lebanon. Both do have myriad ethno-linguistic and religious groups, but Lebanon is occupied by—or under the influence of—Israel, Syria, Iran, the PLO, and earlier, West European and American troops. Outsider efforts inside Afghanistan will backfire.

Before discussing this ideal outcome, it is useful to survey some other outcomes which have been mooted:

1. *The survival of the Republic under the PDPA.* This would be unlikely, in fact virtually impossible, given the destructive and failed pacification efforts, and so much bloodshed. The best hope for leading PDPA cadrés such as Najibullah would be to end up in the USSR. Historical precedents exist for this. When the British withdrew from Afghanistan in 1842 and 1880, they took Afghans who collaborated with them back to British India. Toughing it out in Kabul, PDPA cadrés would probably have a very short life expectancy.

2. *The Interim Government* of the *Islamic Unity of Afghan Mujahideen* reaches Kabul and holds down the fort until elections can be held to a representative body. However, this 'government' represents only a small percentage of the Afghan population. Most observers agree that it was forced on the *Islamic Unity of Afghan Mujahideen* by Pakistan, which wanted an interim government formed before the Geneva Accords were signed. The USA and the USSR jointly rebuffed Pakistan, for both had only one major goal: to get the Soviets' troops out. The *Interim Mujahideen Government* is not expected to survive very long.

3. *The 'War Lord' Gambit.* The fear of some observers is that if post-war refugee-repatriation supplies and reconstruction materials are controlled by local commanders, they will become virtual regional 'War Lords', such as existed in China during the 1930s. Given the patterns of collective leaderships mentioned earlier, this is an improbable scenario.

4. *Afghan army general(s) or other ranks seize Kabul, and invite former King Mohammad Zahir to return and form a government.* The possible role of the former king has been discussed by the Soviets, Americans, Pakistanis, Afghan refugees and almost anyone who has any interest in the Afghan situation. The issue has divided the seven-party *Mujahideen* alliance. In general, non-Pushtun groups have not favoured the return of the

Mohammadzai Durrani former monarch in any capacity. Many non-Durrani Pushtun have felt the same way. The most vocal support for Zahir Shah has come from refugees, living mainly in Europe and North America, who served as high officials during the decade of the constitutional monarchy (1963-73). They look forward to a rebirth of the 'good old days', an impossible dream, for, as mentioned earlier, Afghanistan will never be the same. These Western-oriented bureaucrats and technocrats must accept some of the responsibility for the ultimate leftist takeover in 1978 and Soviet invasion of 1979. During the constitutional period Zahir Shah gave his Western-educated cabinet great latitude to implement the reform programs which, incidentally, they had been talking about for years. But ten years of virtual inactivity resulted, which directly led to Daoud's return. The former ministers blame various members of the royal family for interference, but they cannot so facilely dismiss their failure to act.

Several polls have indicated that the majority of those polled wanted Zahir Shah to return. But these were flawed. Men asked a question by pollsters, non-literate folk (and even literate folk— and I am in this category!) give replies which they assume the pollsters desire. The Afghan refugees, when asked anything about future leadership usually answered 'Zahir Shah', partly because the name 'Zahir Shah' was floating about.

No matter what one feels about Zahir Shah, his personality and accomplishments, he can possibly—just possibly—perform one valuable function over a 24-to-48 hour period. When Afghanistan settles down to a peace, however shaky, the former king could fly into Kabul in a private capacity. He could appear over Kabul TV and announce that in the interest of national unity and in keeping with Afghan culture and history, he proposed to call a national assembly to consider what form an Afghan government should take. He would leave the selection of delegates to the regional power elites, or, alternatively, he could call elections. Having done this, Zahir Shah would then return to Italy to a richly-deserved retirement.

If—and this is a big if—the assembly chose to ask Zahir Shah to return, so be it. The will of the people would have spoken, but I doubt this will happen.

5. *Afghanistan becomes a 'fundamentalist' Islamic state linked with Iran or Pakistan,* or *the Wahabbi of Saudi Arabia gain*

influence in Afghan affairs. The term 'fundamentalist' itself is fundamentally incorrect. Fundamental to what? Most leaders, inside and outside Afghanistan, are not fundamentalists. The term used by Olivier Roy, Islamist, is more acceptable.[11] Few of the Islamist Sunni leaders and only a few Shia want to emulate Khomeini's Iran. Iranians and Afghans are different breeds of the theological cat. As one major Afghan Shia leader put it: 'The Iranians are *Iranian* Shia, and we are *Afghan* Shia'. The Saudis have spent megabucks among the refugees and resistance fighters in attempts to gain converts for their ultra-conservative, reformist brand of Islam, but with little success. The Afghans owe the Saudis a tremendous debt because they were among the first to assist the resistance in the dark, early days of their struggle. Money from the Saudis kept the anti-government revolts alive. The cash enabled the resistance to buy weapons and ammunition from the gun factories of the Federally Administered Tribal Areas of Pakistan. The Saudis also invested deeply in public health facilities, hospitals and schools. Their major impact, however, was on bodies—not minds.

6. *The North-South Partition Gambit*. Some observers with little knowledge of Afghan history and cultural patterns have suggested that the Soviets may continue to occupy Afghanistan north of the Hindu Kush, or leave behind an independent 'Turkistan', tied closely to the Soviet Union. In 1988, a separate Afghan Deputy Prime Ministry for the North was created, and reportedly a new province centered around Sar-i-Pul (gas and oil fields) was separated from the southern parts of Jozjan and Balkh. Also a new province of Nuristan was created in eastern Afghanistan.

Evidence does exist of Soviet plans to retain an influential economic position in the north, which is quite logical. After all, the USSR and Afghanistan have a long common boundary, about 1000 miles, and many Soviet investments in Afghanistan's economic development have been in the north. Soviet projects have been geared to exploitable raw materials which, when developed, could be exported to the USSR. These items include natural gas (oil will be exploited later), coal, copper, iron ore, fertiliser, cement, gold, uranium, and emeralds. Afghanistan's mountainous terrain is honeycombed with exploitable natural resources, and the Soviets will continue to import these items. The Afghans owe large debts to the Soviets who helped the

Afghans develop a number of natural resources—and then helped themselves to the resources.

Sar-i-Pul Province, according to some, could form the basis for a 'Turkistan' nation in the event of Kabul falling to the *Mujahideen*. The new province would be very vulnerable to *Mujahideen* attacks from the foothills and mountains to the south. Long-range rockets and moveable artillery fire would play havoc with any installations on the Turkistan Plains of north Afghanistan.

In addition, the people of north Afghanistan (Tajik, Uzbek, Turkoman, Karakalpack) are vehemently anti-Russian. Virtually the entire populations are the descendants of either refugees from Tsarist oppression and *basmachi* (or the descendants of the *basmachi*) of the anti-Soviet civil wars of the 1920s. Therefore, continued Soviet military occupation of the north (as contrasted to economic activities) would mean continued warfare.

The rest of the partition theory has Afghanistan south of the Hindu Kush going to Pakistan. The Pakistanis, however, desperately want the refugees to go home. All Pakistan needs is another 6-7 million Pushtun, Baluch, and Nuristanis to complicate its already complicated ethnic scene. And most of these proposed male citizens would be well-armed and veterans of a bloody war.

7. *Pakistan attempts to control the situation.* Pakistan was in the front line of the First Russo-Afghan War from the very beginning, and over the years the violence and death inside Pakistan escalated. Pakistan accepted the world's largest single refugee community because most of the refugees had ethno-linguistic and cultural cousins in Pakistan, and because of the Muslim custom of accepting Muslim refugees as a duty. Pakistan always had some influence with the leaders of the *Mujahideen* alliance, mainly because it controlled the flow of military supplies to the parties, who subsequently moved the supplies across the border to their favourite commanders. The government of Pakistan under the late President Zia ul-Haq also had its favourites among the party leaders, the primary one being Gulbuddin Hekmatyar of *Hezb-i Islami*.

It has been rumoured that Pakistan could support a dash for Kabul by a brigade-size unit of *Mujahideen* trained by the Pakistanis to seize power and declare their leaders the *bona fide* government. The leaders would be Hekmatyar and Sayyaf, with

Hekmatyar as military commander and Professor Sayyaf as head religious leader. This would be a mistake, for the Soviets failed to spread their influence over Afghanistan in nine years of trying. The resistance commanders and their men were largely responsible for this, and those around Kabul would probably not welcome attempts by one or two groups from the Pakistan-based alliance to seize power. The commanders would either stop the force as it moved toward Kabul, or destroy it after it reached the city. Efforts by any outsiders, not just Pakistan, to have a decisive outcome on Afghanistan's political future will probably be doomed to failure.

8. *The Cordovez Plan.* Señor Diego Cordovez, Special Representative on Afghanistan to the United Nations Secretary-General, announced his 'peace plan' in Islamabad on 9 July 1988. His plan included three basic suggestions: (a) a *ceasefire*; (b) an interim 'national government for peace and reconstruction', formed after consultation with *all*[12] groups of Afghans, with the chief mission of creating peaceful conditions; (c) a *Loya Jirgah*, called by the interim government, to write a constitution. With the promulgation of a new constitution, the interim government would resign, and its members would have already guaranteed not to participate in the subsequent elections.

A critique is in order. First, a ceasefire is only workable when two armies face each other across definable boundaries or zones, like North and South Korea, India and Pakistan in Kashmir, the Arabs and Israelis. However, in Afghanistan X-number of commanders are scattered throughout the countryside and in the towns and cities, many of whom are regionally independent of any outside control. While certain local commanders made temporary ceasefire agreements with Soviet and PDPA troops at different times in the past, to expect a nationwide ceasefire to work would be fantasy. Second, how would it be possible to create a broad-based government in which *all* segments of the Afghan political scene were represented? Who would select the members? Would it include Shia? Would it include the PDPA? Third, how could one create a *Loya Jirgah* to satisfy all parties? The Pushto term, *Loya Jirgah,* should be stricken from the Afghan political vocabulary, because non-Pushtun groups regard it, rightly or wrongly, as an institution devised to perpetuate Pushtun hegemony. In addition, both Babrak Karmal and Najibullah diluted (and in the view of many,

46

disgraced) the institution, so that it can probably never retain its status.

This brings us to the last possibility, one which may succeed in the long run:

9. *Evolution of an Islamic Federated Republic, based on provincial autonomy or semi-autonomy.* Afghanistan is now going through a genuine revolution, and revolutions (to paraphrase Chairman Mao) are not tea parties. When a revolutionary movement overthrows a government at the centre the result is a bloody transitional period.[13]

But when the political dust has settled and the bodies have been buried, Afghanistan's Islamic Federated Republic will be based on Islamic principles but probably not dominated by conservative religious leaders. The regional *Mujahideen* commanders and the traditional power elite will come together in Kabul to decide the political future. Outside interference from any source will backfire, and the Afghans will solve their problems in their own way—collective leadership, with ultimate elections, of representatives determined by population density.

The autonomous provinces can number anywhere from six to ten, depending on how the leadership defines the ethno-linguistic and ecological zones. Four criteria should be considered in drawing the boundaries, and it may be necessary to re-draw them from time to time. The four are: (a) distribution of major ethno-linguistic groups (not every small group can expect autonomy); (b) river patterns, the flow of hydraulics; (c) lines of communication and commerce between cities, towns and villages; (d) natural resources and regional potential for development. Its foreign policy will be non-aligned with loose ties, which means 'partly aligned' at any given time with one superpower or another. The evolution of the Islamic Federated Republic of Afghanistan will take time, but time is a natural resource the Afghans have in abundance.

The Afghans stopped six centuries of Russian aggression which began with the Principality of Muscovy. Now Moscow has no place to go, and so can look inward and work to achieve Gorbachev's announced goals of *glasnost'* and *perestroika*. I am convinced of two things: the Afghans will decide their own future; and outside interference from any source will be rejected. Influences are already in place, but outside interference will not be tolerated. Ask the Soviets.

47

Table I: **Afghanistan: Estimated Population: 1978-1988**[1]

1978-79

Sedentary Population		12,710,000
Rural	(10,830,000)	
Urban	(1,880,000)	
Semi-Sedentary, Semi-Nomadic		1,500,000
	Total	14,210,000

1987-88

Total estimated population		16,980,000[2]
Minus war dead		1,000,000
Minus Refugees in Pakistan		3,500,000
NWFP	(2,158,000)	
Baluchistan	(818,000)	
Punjab	(180,000)	
Unregistered	(344,000)	
Minus Refugees in Iran		2,000,000
Minus Refugees elsewhere		100,000
	Total minuses	6,600,000

1988

Total population inside Afghanistan:		10,380,000
Settled population		9,380,000
Rural	(6,212,000)	
Urban	(3,168,000)[3]	
Semi-Sedentary, Semi-Nomadic	1,000,000	

1. Based on information from UNHCR, Islamic Republic of Pakistan, Republic of Afghanistan.
2. Based on an estimated population growth of 2%, these figures are what the demography of Afghanistan should have been in 1988, if the war had not intervened.
3. Increased urban growth related to 'internal refugees' fleeing to cities after their villages were destroyed. For example, Kabul expanded from 600,000 in 1978 to 2 million in 1988.

Table II: Reconstruction 1989-1990 (18 months)

Relief-Rehabilitation needs
(in US$ million)

Voluntary Repatriation	**225.4**
Health	8.0
Transport-Logistics	169.4
Water Supply	3.0
Household Goods	5.0
Shelter	22.0
Agricultural Inputs	4.8
Agency Operational Support	13.2
Food Aid*	**335.4**
Repatriation refugees-Internally displaced	239.5
Vulnerable groups	6.1
School children	6.3
Food-for-work program	80.0
Agency Operational Support	3.5
Agriculture, Irrigaton, Rural Development	**332.4**
Agriculture inputs	164.5
Agriculture	56.8
Irrigation	53.1
Rural development	58.0
Social Services	**132.9**
Health programs	37.2
Drugs and medicines	19.0
Water supply	17.7
Education	50.0
Clearance of mines	9.0
Communications, Industry and Power	**129.3**
Transport-Logistics	42.4
Communictions	16.7
Industry	40.3
Power	29.9
Administration and Management	**10.7**
Planning and Statistics	6.0
Project Formulation-Monitoring	1.5
Project Management	0.5
Monuments-Culture Survey	2.7
Total	1,166.1

* Includes ocean freight and overland/inland transport costs amounting to $160.0 million for food aid deliveries to provincial capitals as well as distribution centres inside Afghanistan

Table III: **Estimated Rehabilitation Recovery Needs in Afghanistan (1990-93)**

	Rehabilitation-Recovery needs (in US$ million)
Agriculture, Irrigation, Rural Development	**383.7**
Agricultural inputs	143.0
Agriculture	63.0
Irrigation	104.7
Rural development	73.0
Social Services	**252.6**
Health programs	92.0
Drugs and medicines	68.0
Water supply	61.3
Education	31.3
Communications, Industry and Power	**186.3**
Transport-Logistics	55.3
Communications	41.6
Industry	47.5
Power	41.9
Administration and Management	**17.0**
Planning and Statistics	14.0
Project formulation-monitoring	2.0
Project management	1.0
Total	839.6

FOOTNOTES

1   'Afganistan—predvaritel'nye itogi', *Ogonek*, no.30, 1988.
2   Louis Dupree, 'Cultural Change Among the Mujahidin and Muhajerin,' in Bo Huldt and Erland Jansson (eds.), *The Tragedy of Afghanistan: The Social, Cultural and Political Impact of the Soviet Invasion* (London: Croom Helm, 1988) pp.20-37.
3   Louis Dupree, *Afghanistan* (Princeton: Princeton University Press, 1980) p.417.
4   Nancy Tapper, 'Abd al-Rahman's North-West Frontier: The Pashtun Colonisation of Afghan Turkistan', in Richard Tapper (ed.), *The Conflict of Tribe and State in Iran and Afghanistan* (London: Croom Helm, 1983) pp.233-261.
5   Azam Gul, *The Agricultural Survey of Afghanistan: First Report* (Peshawar: The Swedish Committee for Afghanistan, 1988) p.38.
6   My italics.
7   Dr M.A. Dadfar, 'Psychiatric Problems Among Refugee Afghan Women', *WUFA* (Writers Union of Free Afghanistan), vol.1, no.2, 1986, pp.61-75; Nancy Hatch Dupree, 'Afghan Refugee Women in Pakistan: The Psycho-cultural Dimension', *WUFA* (Writers Union of Free Afghanistan), vol.3, no.1, 1988, pp.34-45.
8   Personal communication with specialists in Peshawar.
9   Personal communication with specialists in Peshawar.
10   Louis Dupree, 'Red Flag Over the Hindu Kush: Part III: Rhetoric and Reforms, or Promises! Promises!', *American Universities Field Staff Reports*, no. 23-Asia, 1980, pp.7-9.
11   See Olivier Roy, *Islam and Resistance in Afghanistan* (Cambridge: Cambridge University Press, 1986).
12   My italics.
13   Several revolutions illustrate this: French, Russian, Chinese, Cuban. The American colonies did *not* have a revolution, but a War for Independence; a horizontal shift of power occurred: one vested interest class (the Americans) replaced another (the British imperialists). The war did not bring about major shifts in a vertical class structure.

4

The Regional Politics of the Afghan Crisis

Amin Saikal

The Soviet invasion of Afghanistan produced a crisis not simply for the Afghan people, but for the regions of South and South-West Asia as well. It confronted the main regional actors—Pakistan, Iran and India—with a new political-strategic situation, to which they reacted in distinctive ways. This situation is now set to change once again with the Soviet withdrawal. This chapter has two objectives. The first is to delineate the factors which shaped the responses of regional states to the Soviet invasion. The second is to assess the likely implications of Soviet withdrawal for the individual regional states in the light of these responses.

The Soviet invasion marked an unparalleled development in Soviet international behaviour outside the Warsaw Pact since World War II. To much of the world it signalled a dramatic and dangerous change in the Soviet approach to resolving international problems. It could be read by all those regional and international forces which had traditionally suspected an inherent expansionist tendency in Soviet foreign policy as concrete proof that their suspicions were well-founded. It shocked the West, especially the United States, which felt that it had been cheated despite the sustained efforts of the Carter Administration to

52

maintain a policy of *détente* with the USSR.[1] It alarmed China, which perceived the Soviet action to be part of an elaborate plan to encircle that country, particularly in the light of the Soviet-backed Vietnamese invasion of Kampuchea a year earlier.[2] It perturbed much of the Third World, most importantly many of its Muslim member states, which saw the Soviet action among other things as an atheist assault on their wider religious interests.

However, apart from the Afghan people, no one was as much affected by the Soviet action as were Afghanistan's neighbours. For the countries of Pakistan, Iran and India, the Soviet invasion seriously changed the regional balance of power, and put them almost overnight in the unenviable position of having to respond to this new development and cope with its consequences in their own particular ways. Their responses, however, came to be formulated not solely on the basis of the needs and aspirations of the Afghan people. Naturally, they also took into account their *own* interests. The responses that they adopted essentially mirrored these particular interests and substantially differed from each other. Pakistan chose to pursue active opposition to the Soviet invasion; the Iranian regime, while condemning the invasion, took a somewhat lower profile; and India made no public condemnation of the invasion.

The Reactions of the Regional States

A number of factors shaped Pakistan's unique response. It shared a long, permeable frontier and extensive cross-border ethnic ties with Afghanistan. This proximity meant that it bore the brunt of the crisis and felt more vulnerable to a perceived threat of 'Soviet expansionism'[3] than any other regional state. This sense of vulnerability was exacerbated by distinctive structural and historical considerations. The first was the chronic fragility of Pakistan's political and social structures, underscored by serious divisions between four main national ethno-linguistic groups (in order of size the Punjabis, Sindis, Pushtuns and Baluchis). This had in the past exposed the country, during its short but turbulent history since its creation in 1947, to several externally-backed secessionist threats, particularly by Pushtuns and Baluchis, who had been supported by Afghanistan in the context of that country's border disputes with Pakistan.[4] The second was the growth of a serious threat to General Zia ul-Haq's Islamic, anti-Soviet, martial law rule from leftist and centre-leftist opposition, headed by the Pakistan People's Party (PPP) of former Prime Minister Zulfiqar Ali Bhutto, whom Zia overthrew in 1977 and who was hanged two years later on charges of complicity in the murder of a political opponent. The third was Pakistan's traditional political and territorial conflict not only with Afghanistan, but also its eastern neighbour and more entrenched regional foe, India. Successive Pakistani governments had always been troubled by the development of what they had perceived as a Moscow-Kabul-New Delhi Axis, given the growth of close friendship between these actors since the mid-1950s, on the one hand, and the 1971 signing of the Indo-Soviet Treaty of Friendship and Cooperation, on the other. This, together with the fact that the Soviets had supported both Afghanistan and India in their disputes with Pakistan, could not but create a sense of paranoia among many Pakistani leaders and prompt them to view the Soviet invasion of Afghanistan as a regional push against Pakistan—a view which gained increasing salience in the light of New Delhi's continued refusal to condemn the Soviet invasion in public.[5] The fourth was Pakistan's sympathy, since the seizure of power by the People's Democratic Party of Afghanistan (PDPA) in the coup of 27 April 1978, with the Afghan Islamic resistance forces (the *Mujahideen*) and its provision of haven to some Afghan refugees, whose numbers grew dramatically after the invasion. Even before the invasion, this had caused the PDPA and Soviets to accuse Pakistan of 'imperialist' interference in Afghanistan's internal affairs, although it was clear that up to the invasion Pakistani (and for that matter international) sympathy for the *Mujahideen* was insubstantial.[6]

Thus, Islamabad had good reasons to become very fearful of the implications of the Soviet invasion for its national integrity and security as well as regional interests. It therefore found itself with little choice but to adopt a stance of active opposition to the invasion by providing greater logistic support for the *Mujahideen* and acting as the main conduit for supply to them of outside arms—which largely became available only when the Soviet invasion generated international sympathy for them. As the resistance managed to arrest the consolidation of Soviet-PDPA

54

rule, Pakistani involvement in the Afghan crisis grew correspondingly.

This whole development, while holding out the prospects of direct Soviet retaliation, prompted Soviet regional and global adversaries, especially China and the United States, to accord Pakistan greater geo-strategic significance. Zia's regime was consequently able to take a frontline anti-Soviet Islamic position and attract growing foreign, mostly American, economic and military aid.

This, plus the international assistance which began to pour into Pakistan for the Afghan refugees and *Mujahideen*, helped Zia to achieve three important things. First, he was able on the one hand to strengthen and sustain his military base of support, and on the other to generate an unprecedented level of economic activity and growth in support of greater domestic stability. Second, he managed to assume a central position in regional power politics and to earn for his regime a larger degree of international respectability than would normally be the case with a regime of that type. Finally, he succeeded in drawing on the first two to demoralise his domestic opponents and neutralise his external critics. As a result, Pakistan secured what one might call *conflict-based* social and economic stability, which reasonably assisted the long-term continuity of General Zia's rule. This, however, could in no way please India, which saw the renewal of US-Pakistan strategic ties and the growth of China-Pakistan friendship as contrary to its own regional and global interests. The Indians, however, were partly responsible for this development because of the way they responded to the Soviet invasion.

India's response, like Pakistan's, essentially reflected its own national peculiarities. First, India could not publicly *condone* the invasion of a neighbouring state by a superpower. To have done so would have earned the opprobrium of all those states which looked to India as a source of moral leadership since the establishment of the Non-Aligned Movement. Second, however, it was not under any threat as a result of the Soviet invasion, since it was territorially distant from Afghanistan. Nor did it have to cope with the traumas of a refugee problem, although a number of Afghan refugees did find their way to Indian cities. Third, although India enjoyed a position of pre-eminence within the Non-Aligned Movement, the Congress (I) Party of Mrs

Indira Gandhi which returned to office immediately following the Soviet invasion enjoyed close friendship with the Soviet Union. Fourth, given its deep-seated disputes with Pakistan, India had traditionally been disposed to take comfort from anything which would increase the difficulties which Pakistan confronted. Fifth, given its own substantial Muslim minority, New Delhi professed concern about Islamic resurgence, highlighted by the rise of Ayatollah Khomeini's Islamic regime in Iran and Zia's Islamic policies in Pakistan. Sixth, in the context of its aspiration to assume an assertive position in the region, India was not keen to see either American involvement in the region or an expansion of Chinese influence through greater ties with Pakistan, and apparently did not grasp that this was precisely what the Soviet invasion would produce.

The conjunction of these factors led India to adopt an utterly self-serving position, in which moral considerations were subordinated to the dictates of pragmatism. It was a twofold position: one dimension was expressed in public while another was allegedly voiced in private conversation with the Kremlin. Its public position was clearly outlined in a speech by the Indian representative, Brajesh Mishra, at the Emergency Session of the United Nations General Assembly on 11 January 1980. The Indian spokesman, in a carefully worded declaration, stated that 'the Soviet Government has assured our Government that its troops went to Afghanistan at the request of the Afghan Government, a request that was first made by President Amin on 26 December 1979 and repeated by his successor on 28 December 1979, and we have been further assured that the Soviet troops will be withdrawn when requested to do so by the Afghan Government. We have no reason to doubt such assurances, particularly from a friendly country like the Soviet Union, with which we have many close ties.'[7] The Indian representative even criticised the General Assembly's discussing the Soviet invasion, and abstained from supporting a resolution— condemning the Soviet action—which was overwhelmingly adopted on the votes of other member states.

The position which India adopted during the Emergency Session provoked considerable amazement, and subsequently Indian officials sought to downplay it and did not reiterate it publicly in nearly as stark terms. For example the Indian Foreign Minister, P.V. Narasimha Rao, speaking in Parliament on 23

January 1980 said that India hoped that ' ... the people of Afghanistan will be able to resolve their internal problems without outside interference ... we are against the presence of foreign troops and bases in any country. We have expressed our hope that Soviet forces will withdraw from Afghanistan.' He also expressed deep concern about 'the induction of arms in the region [a reference to talk at the time of possible American military aid to Pakistan] and the introduction of Great Power confrontation' as a threat to 'the peace and stability of the region including the security of India'.[8]

None the less, as a precursor of India's policy over the following years the original Indian position at the UN proved to be remarkably accurate. India continued to be the only democracy to repeat the Soviet version of events leading to the invasion, and to maintain friendly contacts and high-level cooperation with the Kabul regime. This involved the revival of the Indian-Afghan Joint Economic Commission in early 1982 and the reported deployment of a number of Indian advisers with the Afghan armed forces.[9] While expressing occasional concern about the suffering and dislocation of the Afghan people and admitting some Afghans to refuge in India, New Delhi made a consistent effort to play down the problem of the Afghan refugees. It treated them not as refugees but as those who had left their country voluntarily; it also refused to give support for the Afghan refugees in Pakistan and Iran.[10]

At the same time, New Delhi claimed that privately it had advanced to the Kremlin leadership its opposition to the invasion, and to the use of force to solve international problems. It justified the contradiction between its private and public positions with the claim that quiet diplomacy was more likely to prove effective in procuring a solution to the Afghanistan problem, and that its gentle public response to the invasion gave it standing to press for such a solution in discussions with the USSR.

Iran fell between these two extremes. There were a number of reasons for this, again as a result of Iran's particular situation.

First, Khomeini's Islamic Government had no ideological affection for the Soviet Union, and was naturally inclined to condemn the invasion by a superpower of a neighbouring Muslim state. Second, however, the geopolitical location of Iran, which shared a lengthy border and several ethnic groups with the USSR, made Iran highly vulnerable to the possibility of direct

Soviet pressure; and limited the capacity of the Khomeini regime (as it would have done that of any regime) to respond strongly to the invasion. Third, the Soviet invasion came at a time when the Iranian leadership was beset with growing post-revolutionary turmoil and an intense and bitter power struggle within the ruling party was in the making—broadly between Islamic radicals and Islamic moderates, with Khomeini's support growing for the former. As a result, the invasion became another substantive issue upon which the different elements involved in the power struggle focused in their attempts to secure domestic and international support. The Islamic radicals, headed by Ayatollah Beheshti, a close confidant of Khomeini and Minister of Justice, as well as the head of the Islamic Revolutionary Council (IRC)—Iran's supreme governing body at the time—was less inclined to antagonise the Soviets in the face of their extreme anti-American stance. On the other hand, the Islamic moderates, represented most notably by two other rival members of the IRC, Abolhassan Bani Sadr (who was subsequently elected as the first President of Iran), and Sadeq Qudbzadeh (who was soon appointed as Foreign Minister), wanted to focus greater attention on the Soviet invasion, partly in order to counterbalance the anti-American extremism of their opponents.[11] Complicating the situation further was the fact that the invasion took place less than two months after the occupation of the American Embassy in Teheran and the taking of the embassy's personnel as hostages by Islamic militants, precipitating a major crisis between Iran and the United States. Although the Islamic radicals gained political ascendency by mid-1981, the protracted power struggle and the hostage crisis overshadowed the Afghanistan problem from the Iranian point of view. Fourth, the outbreak of war with Iraq in September 1980 provided a further distraction which was to persist long after the hostage crisis was resolved. The war of course won priority over most other claimants to regime attention, and resources which might otherwise have been deployed to aid the Afghans' struggle were devoted to the longest and most expensive war in the history of the Middle East. Fifth, Iranian sympathy was particularly directed to those elements within the Afghan resistance which were either avowedly pro-Iranian or anti-American, cutting the Iranians off from the mainstream of the resistance.

All these in combination with the growing regional and global isolation of Iran restricted Teheran's capacity to provide very much more than verbal condemnation of the invasion, or limited material support for the *Mujahideen* and the estimated two million Afghan refugees in Iran.

Regional Relationships after the Invasion

The diverse responses of the regional states affected the relations of those states not simply with the Soviet Union and the Kabul regime, but also with the United States, China, and each other. Pakistan's firm position put it at odds with Moscow and Kabul, but strengthened the foundation for much closer relations not only with the Afghan resistance but also with Beijing, Washington and important Muslim circles in the Middle East, which found it beneficial to assist the country as much as possible. While there are no hard data available on the exact amount of aid from China and moderate-conservative, especially oil-rich, Arab states, the American economic and military assistance proved to be substantial. The first package of aid, concluded in September 1981, amounted to $3.2 billion over the next four years; and the second package negotiated in 1987 for a period of six years amounted to $4 billion.[12]

This markedly strengthened Pakistan's position, something which India found gravely perturbing, although the character of its response to the invasion meant that it was substantially the architect of its own problems. Ironically, until the first substantial American package of aid to Pakistan was agreed upon over twenty months after the invasion, India still had the option to dispel the impression that it was really siding with the Soviets. Its failure to do so left Islamabad with the feeling that there was a coalition between New Delhi and Moscow against Pakistan. It also prompted Washington to conclude that New Delhi was so sympathetic to the USSR that little cost to the USA could result from a substantial increase in aid to Pakistan. Moreover, it furthered Beijing's distrust of India, with which China has had long-standing border and political disputes. Thus, the Indian response to the invasion did not simply assist Pakistan to emerge as a more powerful regional actor than ever before. It also furthered American involvement in the region; dampened the prospects for regional cooperation; and killed for the foreseeable future the long-desired joint Soviet-Indian objective of transforming the Indian Ocean into a 'Zone of Peace' in support of India's naval and therefore regional paramountcy.[13]

The regional relationships of Khomeini's regime were less affected by the invasion than were those of India and Pakistan. It certainly made the specific claim that the presence of Soviet forces in Afghanistan was an obstacle to the development of relations with Moscow. However, given its poor relations with the PDPA regime even before the invasion, its deep contempt for Washington, and its other preoccupations, its relations with Moscow, Islamabad (in spite of the latter's acquisition of American aid), and New Delhi were only to a limited extent affected by events in Afghanistan.

Future Developments

The distinctive considerations which determined the responses of the individual regional states to the Soviet invasion, and the adjustments to regional and international relations which these responses produced, partly set the parameters within which the effects of Soviet withdrawal from Afghanistan will be felt. However, the *regional* effects of withdrawal will also be determined by two other variables. The first variable concerns the possible changes which in the meantime may occur in the policy positions of the regional states. In Pakistan, the political scenery has been changed by the mid-August 1988 death, in a suspicious air crash, of President Zia ul-Haq, who was regarded as the most staunch outside supporter of the *Mujahideen*, and especially the radical *Hezb-i Islami* of Gulbuddin Hekmatyar; and by the appointment of Benazir Bhutto—daughter of Zulfiqar Ali Bhutto—as Prime Minister of Pakistan following the November 1988 elections. In Iran, many changes could emanate from the Iranian regime's increased turn to pragmatism, as manifested in its ceasefire with Iraq and its desire to put an end to its regional and international isolation. In India, a change could arise from Prime Minister Rajiv Gandhi's growing domestic problems, from which he may seek to divert attention by seeking foreign policy successes which might strengthen India's position as the leading actor in the region. The second variable is the precise character of developments in Afghanistan in the aftermath of the Soviet troop pullout. One can envisage quite a number of developments in the medium to longer term, with diverse regional implications. While it is difficult to canvass all, three broad scenarios can be examined, with different degrees of plausibility.

The first is the fall of the PDPA regime in favour of a reasonably stable *Mujahideen*-led Islamic government. Such a development would have both pluses and minuses for Pakistan. On the positive side, Afghanistan would at last be under a regime with broad national legitimacy and international credibility to generate and foster the necessary conditions for a considerable degree of domestic stability and reconstruction. Given the inextricable ethnic, linguistic, religious and geographical ties between Afghanistan and Pakistan as well as the gratitude that a majority of the Afghans, and the *Mujahideen* in particular, feel towards Pakistan because of its general support for the Afghan cause, such a regime in the final analysis would be prone to maintain good friendship with Pakistan.

As long as there is a regime in Islamabad which is not hostile to the *Mujahideen*—and Benazir Bhutto has confirmed her predecessor's policy on Afghanistan—the return of relative stability in Afghanistan could benefit Pakistan in several important ways. First, a significant proportion of the Afghan refugee population in Pakistan would be voluntarily repatriated. Second, the victory of the *Mujahideen* and repatriation of the refugees could be presented by the Pakistan armed forces, which under Zia figured centrally in the formulation of a strong pro-*Mujahideen* stand, as a vindication of their policies. Third, it could put to rest the long-standing border dispute between Afghanistan and Pakistan, for a *Mujahideen*-led government is most unlikely to raise this issue again. Fourth, on the whole, Pakistan would become largely free of the Afghanistan problem and would therefore be positioned to devote greater energy to other foreign policy issues, most importantly, Indo-Pakistan relations. Fifth, it would substantially weaken the Afghanistan problem as an important issue in Pakistan's domestic politics. The Afghanistan factor has so far been extensively used in both ideological and pragmatic ways by different forces—ranging from the centre-right, led by the Muslim League, to the centre-left, headed by the PPP—as a basis for discrediting one another in their competitive quest for power. Thus, under this scenario, a resolution of the Afghan conflict could also contribute to the lessening of internal divisions in Pakistan and foster the development of wider national-political harmony and stability in that country.

However, on the negative side, it would weaken the justification for US economic and military assistance to Pakistan; and would end to all intents and purposes the flow of international aid which has been pouring into Pakistan for the Afghan refugees. This would be particularly so if American-Soviet relations continue to improve. A downward turn in such aid could confront the Pakistan government, irrespective of its ideological leaning, with marked economic and military problems, and with difficult foreign policy choices. It would also expose Pakistan to much more vigorous scrutiny from the US Congress over its nuclear energy programme.

Of course, it must be noted that the development of this scenario will depend very much on two considerations. The more important is the ability of the mainstream of the *Mujahideen* to foster unity by marginalising their extreme elements, some of whose single-minded Islamic radicalism in pursuit of personal leadership ambitions has been held largely responsible not simply for many of the divisions within the ranks of the *Mujahideen*, but also for Soviet and Indian apprehension about the formation of a *Mujahideen*-led government in Kabul.[14] Less important but also helpful would be a consensus on the part of Moscow, Washington, Islamabad and New Delhi that a *Mujahideen*-led government offers the best option to resolve the Afghan problem.

On balance, the first of these seems more achievable now than ever before, for several reasons. The late President Zia has gone, leaving his favoured *Mujahideen* clients in a fairly debilitated position. At the same time, there are signs of greater cooperation between other influential resistance forces and, most importantly, their field commanders. The largest, most professional and least dogmatic *Mujahideen* group, the *Jamiat-i Islami* under Professor Burhanuddin Rabbani, to which also belongs the most celebrated *Mujahideen* commander, Ahmad Shah Massoud, has been active in bolstering such cooperation.

The prospects for an international consensus also seem to be improving. The December 1988 talks in Saudi Arabia between the USSR and the *Mujahideen* leadership may well be the first step in this direction, although New Delhi has yet to abandon its longstanding hostility to the *Mujahideen*. Such consensus would markedly improve the prospects of a reasonable resolution of the conflict. It could also pave the way for a dramatic reduction in regional tensions and a development of a situation which could potentially improve Soviet relations with Iran and Pakistan, as well as China, whose friendship with Pakistan would ultimately have to take into account the effect that Soviet withdrawal might bear on Pakistan.

This is not, however, what India hitherto has deemed to be in the best of its perceived interests. India would of course be pleased by any loosening of ties between Washington and Islamabad, and by closer US scrutiny of Pakistan's nuclear programme. On the other hand, it has remained largely a prisoner of its original stand in response to the Soviet invasion and its growing desire to achieve a position of regional paramountcy. For New Delhi, the factors which motivated it to avoid a public condemnation of the Soviet invasion and to maintain friendly ties with the PDPA regime would obstruct close ties with a *Mujahideen*-led government. New Delhi did not want an Islamic government in Afghanistan then, and does not want one now, even though it may ultimately be forced to come up with various rationalisations for accepting one.

It was precisely because of this that in February 1988, the Indian Defence Minister, on an official visit to Moscow, affirmed with General Secretary Gorbachev 'a mutual interest in Afghanistan as an independent, non-aligned and neutral state *that is friendly to the Soviet Union and India*.'[15] Rajiv Gandhi subsequently confirmed this position by being the first leader outside the Soviet bloc to host an official visit from PDPA leader Najibullah in May, and by stating his preference for Najibullah's regime during his own visit to the United Nations in the following month. In an interview on 11 June, Gandhi categorically stated: 'We ourselves feel that Najibullah is far more preferable for the region to the sort of fanatic fundamentalists who are the alternatives'. This statement he justified with a rhetorical reference to the problems that India could face from the rise of 'Islamic fundamentalism'.[16] This justification was simplistic for two reasons. First, the distinctively ethno-tribally decentralised nature of the Sunni-dominated Afghan society means that 'fundamentalism' is extremely unlikely to take root.[17] Second, recent changes in Iranian behaviour highlight the way in which pragmatic needs can prompt the deradicalisation of 'fundamentalist' regimes.

What one can gather from this is that the renewal of strategic ties between Islamabad and Washington has not been the major consideration in New Delhi's policy formulation. Had this been India's major concern, it would have actively sought to encourage the emergence of a stable popular government through a process of free self-determination in Afghanistan. Its concern is rather to see Pakistan tied down by the burdens of a persisting war in Afghanistan, with the prospect that US aid to Pakistan might in any case fall following Soviet withdrawal.

As for Iran, the country's changing circumstances would oblige it to welcome a stable *Mujahideen*-led government, although its natural preference would be for the Shi'ite minority rather than the Sunni groups which would be certain to dominate any such regime. The major obstacle which it has identified to warmer relations with Moscow would necessarily be removed, although this does not of course mean that a change in Afghanistan would lead to a greater degree of Soviet influence in Iran given the wider policy options now plainly figuring in Teheran's calculus of decision.

A second scenario, which seems increasingly remote, could be grounded in Soviet moves to *afghanise* the war, and to ensure its continuation until an exhausted opposition agreed to the formation of a government committed to respecting what the USSR asserts to be its interests. Under such a scenario, the Soviets' termination of their direct combat involvement in Afghanistan would be compensated by an extensive Soviet logistic, equipment and advisory support for the PDPA—something which would not be in violation of the Geneva Accords. This scenario, if it eventuated, would bring little relief to Pakistan and Iran. They would be left with the burdens of the continuing war—the refugees would certainly not return. Yet at the same time, the presence of Soviet forces in Afghanistan could no longer be cited as a justification for continued American aid to Pakistan. Consequently, this is the scenario which, in the absence of a thoroughly secure PDPA, New Delhi would value the most. India has frequently voiced its readiness to help the Soviets in this respect. While New Delhi has refrained from specifying the ways in which it could extend this help, unofficial

Indian logistic and advisory support on a considerable scale cannot be ruled out.

The third scenario envisages Afghanistan's collapsing into anarchy, with numerous centres of power competing within the country. Given the heterogeneous nature of both Afghan society and the resistance, whose commanders and units have operated very much from distinct territorial bases, as well as the irresponsibility of which regional and global powers are capable, this is a scenario which cannot be discounted. Such a scenario would provide opportunities for different outside forces to act as patrons for client-groups within Afghanistan, for reasons of self-interest and with a view to denying openings to other patron powers. This would to an extent re-create the conditions which applied in Afghanistan for much of the nineteenth century, when the country existed by and large in a state of political and social disarray within different principalities; and could neutralise it as a state-actor in the region. This raises all sorts of imponderable questions about the long term future of the region, which can only be addressed in a broader global framework. It is a scenario from which no regional or international actor (except possibly New Delhi) could obtain much delight, and the consequences for the Afghan people would be horrific.

As the situation stands, the future of Afghanistan remains uncertain, and so are the future consequences of the Soviet withdrawal from that country and the reaction of regional actors to these consequences. Whatever Soviet designs may have been to ensure the position of the PDPA, even senior Soviet officials have voiced doubts that the regime could survive for long. In the event of the first scenario's materialising, Soviet withdrawal, marking an historic degradation of Soviet power-projection capability to its south, would prove beneficial in helping to foster conditions for greater stability in the region. However, should the second or third scenarios eventuate, the Afghanistan crisis would continue to rob the regional states of chances to engage in substantial confidence-building measures to promote greater regional harmony and autonomy in world politics. Rightly or wrongly, India has taken upon itself an important role in the Afghanistan conflict. Should it fail to manage this role properly, it will have a lot for which to answer. The *Mujahideen* already feel a deep resentment towards India, and in the case of further Indian mismanagement, New Delhi will have little ground for complaint when a future non-communist government in Afghanistan declines to accept it as worthy of trust.

FOOTNOTES

1 See Jimmy Carter, *Keeping Faith: Memoirs of a President* (London: Collins, 1982) pp.471-472.
2 See R.K.I. Quested, *Sino-Russian Relations* (London: George Allen & Unwin, 1984) pp.154-156.
3 *Time*, 28 January 1980. On the background to Pakistan's reaction, see also W. Howard Wriggins, 'Pakistan's Foreign Policy after Afghanistan', in Stephen Philip Cohen (ed.), *The Security of South Asia: American and Asian Perspectives* (Urbana and Chicago: University of Illinois Press, 1987) pp.61-80.
4 See D. Mukerjee, 'Afghanistan under Daud: Relations with Neighboring States', *Asian Survey*, vol.15, no.4, April 1975, pp.301-312.
5 Personal interviews with senior Pakistani officials in Islamabad in late December 1983.
6 J. Bruce Amstutz, *Afghanistan: The First Five Years of Soviet Occupation* (Washington, D.C.: National Defense University Press, 1986) pp.202-203.
7 For the full text of Mishra's statement see UN General Assembly, Sixth Emergency Special Session, *Provisional Verbatim Record of the Third Meeting*, Document (A/ES-6/PV.3, General Assembly, United Nations, 11 January 1980).
8 *Foreign Affairs Record* (New Delhi), January 1980, p.19.
9 Yossef Bodansky, 'New pressures on key Indian borderlands', *Jane's Defence Weekly*, 30 April 1988, pp.840-842, at p.840.
10 Thomas Perry Thornton, 'India and Afghanistan' in Theodore L. Eliot, Jr. and Robert L. Pfaltzgraff, Jr. (eds.), *The Red Army on Pakistan's Border: Policy Implications for the United States* (Washington: Pergamon-Brassey's, 1986) pp.44-70, at p.61.
11 See Amin Saikal, 'Khomeini's Iran', *Current Affairs Bulletin*, vol.60, no.5, October 1983, pp.18-30, at pp.26-27.
12 *Keesing's Record of World Events*, vol.33, no.3, March 1987, p.34995.
13 For a detailed discussion see Walter K. Anderson and Leo E. Rose, 'Superpowers in the Indian Ocean: The Goals and Objectives', in The International Peace Academy (ed.), *The Indian Ocean As A Zone of Peace* (The Netherlands: Martinus Nijhoff Publishers, 1986) pp. 1-47.
14 For details see Olivier Roy, *Islam and Resistance in Afghanistan* (Cambridge: Cambridge University Press, 1986) pp.110-138.
15 *Pravda*, 12 February 1988, pp.1-2. My italics.
16 Elaine Sciolino, 'Gandhi Faults Islamic Rule for Kabul', *The New York Times*, 11 June 1988, p.4.
17 For a detailed discussion of Islam in Afghanistan, see Roy, *op.cit.*

5

The Afghan Conflict and Soviet Domestic Politics

T.H. Rigby

After nine years of active combat Soviet troops have withdrawn from Afghanistan without having achieved the political and military objectives for which they were sent there. Their primary objectives may be summarised as defeating the anti-communist insurgency and firmly installing a communist regime under effective Soviet control. Secondary objectives included advancing the Soviet military frontier a thousand kilometres to the South and to within five hundred kilometres of the Arabian Sea, and demonstrating, as in Hungary in 1956 and Czechoslovakia in 1968, that the USSR will not tolerate satellite regimes in neighbouring states being overthrown and the transition to 'socialism' being reversed. The cost of the Afghanistan enterprise was a major one on several counts. Its purely military costs were kept to a relatively modest level, as Geoffrey Jukes's analysis in Chapter Six shows, and there was doubtless some useful learning. Its costs for Soviet foreign relations, however, both *vis-à-vis* the Western alliance and the Third World, were profoundly and almost unrelievedly negative. Against this background, withdrawal without having achieved the initial objectives must be counted as a major political and military defeat for the USSR.

Such defeats may have an enormous political impact at home. One has only to recall the role of Russia's failures in the Crimean War as a catalyst for the Great Reforms of the 1860s, including the abolition of serfdom, or in the Russo-Japanese War, which led via the 1905 Revolution to the (sadly aborted) beginnings of a liberal constitutional order. Even the cataclysmic impact of World War I, although this seems to be attenuating the analogy egregiously, has a certain relevance which will not have been lost on the more nervous conservatives within the Soviet bureaucracy. Russia, of course, is hardly peculiar in suffering domestic political consequences from military-political failures abroad, but the autocratic character of its regimes has historically exerted a multiplier effect on these consequences. The French withdrawal from Algeria and the American withdrawal from Vietnam, perhaps the closest foreign analogies in recent decades, certainly had a substantial domestic impact, in the former case at least one of lasting significance. Yet these had nothing like the consequences for the socio-political order of the Russian cases cited.

Nevertheless, in my view the withdrawal from Afghanistan is unlikely to have persistent and deep-going domestic political implications in the USSR itself. The most obvious reason for this is that the war has impacted far less massively and obviously on the Soviet population than did the Algerian and Vietnam wars on the French and American populations respectively, not to mention the Crimean and Japanese wars on the ordinary people of Russia. This is due as much to the media monopoly enjoyed by the Soviet regime and the organisational and coercive resources at its disposal to protect it and its policies from serious public criticism, as it is to the relatively modest scale and the geographical and psychological remoteness of its involvement. That said, one must immediately add that the withdrawal will undoubtedly have, is indeed already having, some significant consequences within the USSR, and these on a number of levels.

In the short to middle term it will bring a number of substantial benefits. Most obviously, there will be the savings to the Soviet economy. Although the cost of waging the war has not, perhaps, been all that large in relation to the total military budget, it has been escalating and would have had to escalate further if there were to be any chance of a decisive victory over the *Mujahideen*. The Gorbachev leadership clearly aims at curbing military expenditure during the difficult period of restructuring the economic system, and getting out of Afghanistan, like scrapping intermediate range missiles, will contribute to this.

If the Soviet withdrawal has implications for *perestroika*, so it does for *glasnost'* too. If they had decided to soldier on in Afghanistan, the freer flow of information to which they are committed, particularly in the press and electronic media, would inevitably have amplified negative public awareness of the war more and more, unless of course it were treated as a special case calling for old-style distortion and censorship—which is, by the way, largely how it is treated even now—in which case the whole *glasnost'* operation would be discredited.

A more basic reason why withdrawal is politically advantageous is that the war was becoming more and more unpopular as the casualties mounted and victory seemed no closer.[1] Eastern Europe is a poor analogy here, since it is from that direction that Russians see the primary threat to their security, and most would probably want their government to hold fast in any combat situation there. Nor, despite China's support for the Afghan resistance, is their relationship such as to touch off the anti-China paranoia widespread among the Russian population. No doubt some ideological conservatives, for whom the 'Brezhnev doctrine' is a direct corollary of the sacrosanct principle of 'proletarian internationalism', find the desertion of an embattled 'fraternal' regime hard to stomach, but such dogmatic notions cut little ice with the general public. Among the right-wing nationalists some must certainly see the withdrawal as a betrayal of Russia's imperial destiny, but others will welcome it, because they resent Russian lives and treasure being squandered on unworthy and ungrateful Third World elites.[2] As for the non-Russian half of the Soviet population, they can only welcome the cessation of sacrifices exacted from them in furtherance of Moscow's imperial ambitions. It was, then, a predominantly unpopular war, and governments that disengage from unpopular wars usually gain political credit, at least in the short run.

Theory and Ideology

As for the middle-to-long run, I shall be coming back to that later, but first I want to consider the implications of the

69

withdrawal for another level of Soviet political life, namely the theoretical or ideological level.

All rulers operate in the context of clusters of ideas which justify their power and inform their policies. What is peculiar about the Soviet Union and other communist-ruled states is the comprehensive and systematic character of the legitimating world-view and its claim to give the only truly scientific account of all aspects of human affairs. All policy, including foreign policy, is supposed to be scientifically based (*nauchno obosnovana*) and there is a literature relating to every policy field which purports to demonstrate this scientific basis, a literature emanating from groups of specialist scholars and 'ideological workers'. Now, it is quite true that in practice the proclaimed 'theoretical basis' of policy often amounts to little more than *ex post facto* justification of decisions made on entirely pragmatic grounds, and that, arguably, is one respect in which Soviet politics is not so different from anyone else's politics. It is also true that Soviet policy-oriented theory, especially in the Stalin era, but not only then, is often intellectually primitive, giving the impression of a pompously dogmatic and vacuous pseudo-science. Nevertheless it would be a mistake to dismiss it as irrelevant to political action. Marxism-Leninism provides leaders and scholar-ideologists alike with their essential vocabulary for describing social realities, and thereby substantially governs their perceptions of these realities. To sum up: much emphasis is placed on the scientific basis of Soviet policy, groups of specialists are engaged in policy-related studies articulated in terms of Marxist-Leninist concepts, and these studies are relevant to policy development.

It is important to make these points, as they are pertinent both to the decision to commit Soviet troops to Afghanistan and to the decision to withdraw them, while at the same time the Afghanistan experience is clearly having a feed-back effect on the theoretical understandings associated with these decisions.

Soviet policy towards the Third World since World War II has undergone a number of sharp twists and turns. Under Stalin its key determinants were a 'two-camp' ('socialist' versus 'imperialist'), zero-sum view of world politics, combined with marked caution as to direct Soviet involvement in 'anti-imperialist' struggles. The rise to power of the ebullient Khrushchev coincided with a phase of economic and military-technological dynamism (*sputnik* and the like) in the USSR and an acceleration of the decolonisation process in the world at large, and in this context a more active and optimistic Third World policy emerged. The nuclear 'balance of terror' between the Soviet and 'imperialist' camps was seen as calling for a shift to peaceful (though competitive) coexistence between East and West, while at the same time sharply reducing the risks attending direct Soviet involvement with the newly independent countries, with the aim of coopting them into a single Soviet-led 'anti-imperialist' movement and encouraging their gradual transition to 'socialism'.

The Khrushchevian hubris evaporated in the wake of the Cuban missile crisis, the break with China and the collapse of Soviet influence in a number of newly independent countries. Without discarding the commitment to competitive peaceful coexistence and to the belief that in the long haul the ex-colonial countries would gravitate to 'socialism', the Soviet leadership became alarmed at the dangers of unintended nuclear war while at the same time suffering a sharp drop in confidence in their capacity to control the international communist movement, let alone developments in the non-aligned countries. Khrushchev now placed prime emphasis on improving East-West relations and curbed Soviet activities in the Third World.[3]

Despite some changes of rhetoric, Khrushchev's successors did not at first depart substantially from these positions, and it was not till the early 1970s that a new upsurge of optimism and activism emerged. The United States was now seen as a declining power, the correlation of forces as moving decisively in favour of 'socialism', and the Third World as entering a new era of revolutionary change. In this context the Brezhnev regime sought with a measure of success to combine a policy of superpower *détente* with escalation of Soviet involvement, often including military involvement, in radical Third World States, with a view to drawing them decisively into the Soviet orbit.[4] This new adventurism, however, proved even more short-lived than the Khrushchevian equivalent of two decades earlier. Soviet economic decline, the revival of Western economic and technological dynamism, the restoration of American confidence and firmness, and the failure of the USSR's new 'socialist' clients in the Third World, despite massive military aid, to consolidate their power and defeat Western-backed insurgents, all contributed to a new pessimism, a reluctance to undertake new

71

involvements, and a concentration of effort on holding the line, on preventing the demise of their 'socialist' and 'socialist-oriented' clients at the hands of the 'counter-revolutionaries'.[5] This orientation was already apparent in Brezhnev's last years, and has persisted throughout the eighties. A version of it has become an integral part of Gorbachev's 'new political thinking'.

Now, all these shifts of policy towards the Third World reflect decisions taken at the highest political level, but they were decisions adopted in a context of information and ideas largely created by the leaders' foreign affairs advisers, scholars and ideologists. These 'foreign affairs influentials' are to be found on leaders' personal staffs, in the Central Committee apparatus, the Foreign Affairs Ministry, among political journalists, and in Academy of Sciences 'think-tanks'. Their character and role have greatly changed over the years. Under Stalin they were few in number and limited in influence. Since then there has been a virtually uninterrupted process of expanding numbers, widening access to information, in particular from Western sources, greater diversity of views and freedom of specialist debate and public discussion, and the growing influence of well-trained and intellectually sophisticated area specialists, most of them working in such 'think-tanks' as the Institute of World Economy and International Relations (IMEMO), the Institute of the USA and Canada, The Institute on the Economics of the World Socialist System, and the Institute of Oriental Studies.

Afghanistan in Soviet Third-World Policy

All this is by way of background, but it is very important background for estimating the likely impact of the Afghanistan experience on Soviet Third World policy and its intellectual underpinnings. Without going into detail, the history of Soviet relations with Afghanistan can be seen as following fairly closely the periodisation of Soviet Third World policy I have just outlined. Stalin avoided direct involvement, and was satisfied with Afghan neutrality. Khrushchev took advantage of shared hostility towards Pakistan and other overlapping foreign policy interests to foster cooperation with the Afghan government during Mohammad Daoud's premiership, and in 1955 began the provision of military aid. However, it was not till the Brezhnev phase of Third World activism in the early-to-mid 1970s that substantial Soviet involvement in Afghanistan's internal affairs emerged, following the success of Daoud's coup in 1973, with some help from pro-Soviet leftists. The seizure of power by the Marxist-Leninist People's Democratic Party of Afghanistan in April 1978, whether or not the Soviet Union had a direct hand in it, was the culmination of this process of growing Soviet influence in Afghan political life, especially in the military.

There are other respects, too, in which Afghanistan fits the general pattern of Soviet Third World Policy during the 1970s. The Brezhnev regime, following a long series of disappointments in Soviet relations with 'bourgeois nationalist' regimes, now concentrated their main attention on states of 'socialist orientation', with revolutionary leaders prepared (as the Cuban Castro regime had been) to set up and rule through Soviet-type vanguard parties, in which the Communist Party of the Soviet Union (CPSU) sought to establish a strong influence. For the most part these turned out to be less developed countries (Ethiopia, Angola, South Yemen) rather than those ruled by the Soviet Union's actual or former 'bourgeois nationalist' friends (Egypt, Indonesia, India, Syria).[6] This policy shift evolved in the context of wide-ranging discussions among Soviet Third-World specialists. However, some specialists probably had misgivings about it from the start, and these were soon finding expression in scholarly publications. They suggested that quite specific conditions might be necessary for a country to jump successfully from a feudal or pre-feudal society to socialism, by-passing capitalism. They argued the importance of the cultural and structural peculiarities of particular countries, and they warned against 'leftist' miscalculations that could lead to debacles. Developments on the ground lent force to these arguments. The revolutionary leaders and their vanguard parties turned out in most cases to enjoy a very narrow basis of support and found themselves confronted with large scale revolts, assisted to be sure from outside but possessing a strong indigenous support which they were unable to crush. In the late 1970s and through the 1980s there was wide-ranging discussion of these issues in the specialist literature[7] and it was in this context that the Soviet leadership shifted to a far more cautious policy, a policy of assisting their existing clients in the Third World to stay afloat, but avoiding getting embroiled with new ones.

73

The one major difference between the course of Soviet policy towards Afghanistan and its other recently-acquired clients was obviously the direct involvement of the Soviet armed forces. In these other cases Soviet backing was limited to providing advisers, military supplies, economic aid and training. Cuban troops were used against their clients' rivals, but never Soviet ones. Nevertheless, the introduction of combat troops into Afghanistan should probably not be seen as contradicting the more cautious policy towards Third World involvements, which was already emerging in the late 1970s. It is sufficiently explained by the imminent danger of Afghanistan falling into the hands of political forces actively hostile to the USSR, for the first time in Soviet history, and the lack of other means to prevent this.

The withdrawal of Soviet forces from Afghanistan without their having achieved their objective of eliminating this danger will obviously have large implications for the Soviet Union's Third World alliance system generally, and these are explored by Dr Miller in Chapter Seven. What I want to point out here is that there are important theoretical implications as well. Those scholars who warned against close Soviet involvement with self-proclaimed Marxist regimes in poorly developed countries now see their arguments as vindicated by events. The 'I told you so's' and recriminations have already begun. Academician Oleg Bogomolov has recently declared that his Institute on the Economics of the World Socialist System had considered at the time that the intervention was mistaken, and said as much in an unsolicited brief to the Brezhnev leadership.[8] Nodari Simoniia of the Institute of Oriental Studies, recalling his twelve-year-long struggle to draw attention to the erroneous assumptions underlying the up-beat Third World policies of the 1970s, against the too-powerful opposition of a group of policy-advisers and specialists led by R.A. Ul'ianovskii, Deputy Head of the Central Committee's International Department, has acidly remarked that if Ul'ianovskii had spent less time attacking his (Simoniia's) theoretical position, but instead, 'had directed his efforts to comprehending its applicability to, for example, the situation that developed in Afghanistan after 1978, then possibly neither the Afghan nor the Soviet people would have undergone all they have.'[9] And Major-General K.M. Tsagolov stated with admirable frankness in an interview in July 1988, 'To put it

74

briefly, I was convinced that on 27 April 1978 a military coup (*perevorot*) had occurred which had the potential possibilities of developing into a national-democratic revolution. Unfortunately, this did not happen. We became the victims of our own illusions.'[10]

Soviet scholars and ideologists are now faced with the task of defining the precise lessons to be drawn from the Afghanistan experience. Was it only the military intervention that was wrong, or did the chief error lie in the April 1978 revolution? Or were the roots of the problem further back still, in the 1973 coup of Mohammad Daoud? Should Third World countries avoid forced marches to socialism and develop instead a largely free-enterprise market economy, and if so should this be more analogous to Lenin's NEP, with a Marxist vanguard party in charge and a strong state sector, or to such 'newly industrialising countries' as Thailand, Taiwan or even South Korea? Or is there some further alternative?.

Some Soviet specialists no doubt see wider theoretical implications as well. One may or may not agree with Daniel Papp's contention that progressive revisions of Soviet theory relating to Third World development could undermine major elements in Soviet Marxist-Leninist ideology generally.[11] However, such revisions are likely to resonate with and reinforce current challenges to the established dogma on social and political development in the Soviet Union itself, including the historical necessity of the bureaucratic command economy, forced collectivisation, and the bureaucratisation of the party itself.

The Political Impact of the Afghanistan Experience

Afghanistan has been a painful learning experience for the Soviet leadership no less than for their specialist advisers and ideologists. Gorbachev and his colleagues have sought to distance themselves from the decision to intervene, implying it resulted from the pernicious conditions and atmosphere of Brezhnev's 'period of stagnation'. Soviet Foreign Minister Shevardnadze, speaking in Madrid in January 1988, said that 'the pain of Afghanistan is our pain too', and he added, 'Not having chosen this legacy for ourselves (but) accepting it for what it is,

75

we are also obliged to take decisions as to how to deal with it from here on'.[12] Failure in Afghanistan, along with the dismal record of Soviet-supported radical regimes in Africa and elsewhere, will perhaps encourage Soviet leaders to take more notice in future of those specialists who point out the obstacles and uncertainties attending any attempt to effect radical political and social change in Third World countries.

But will it have any direct impact on the power and prestige of individual Soviet leaders? So far Gorbachev and his supporters have avoided laying any personal blame for the unasked-for legacy, at least publicly. It is sometimes suggested that Afghanistan may be yet another nail in the political coffins of those older Politburo members who had a hand in the decision to send in Soviet troops, but who knows: even Gorbachev may have good reason not to want too much exposure of just what was said and done by individual leaders at the end of the Brezhnev era. On the other hand, the decision to withdraw could well become a subject of recrimination if things come badly unstuck in Afghanistan. In this case it would probably figure just as one issue among many, and probably not the most important one, so its impact on Gorbachev's position would doubtless depend largely on how well or badly his policies generally were faring. All the same, the withdrawal obviously involves not only international but also domestic political risks for Gorbachev and his supporters.

Finally, I should like to offer some brief observations on possible middle to longer-term effects of the Afghanistan experience on political attitudes among the Soviet population. Here, one may identify two factors, at least, that could assume some importance.

The first is the Afghan veteran, the *voin-internatsionalist* (soldier-internationalist) to use the official euphemism, or as the ordinary Russian would call him, the *afganets*. There are now some hundreds of thousands of *afgantsy*, and there has been much in their experience to bind them together and set them apart from their fellow citizens. Combat against Muslim freedom-fighters among a largely hostile population turned out to be utterly different from the war their fathers had fought against the Germans and the war for which their whole education and conditioning had prepared them. On top of this, for many years they had felt forgotten and neglected by their country: they were rarely mentioned in the official media because the Soviet leaders wanted to play down the role of the USSR's so-called 'limited contingent' for political reasons, both domestic and international. As Geoffrey Jukes points out, this even applied to the military press, although the military publishing house published some rousing tales of derring-do against the treacherous *dushmany* ('enemies').[13] It was only with the flowering of *glasnost'* in 1986 that the virtual news black-out was breached and there were more and more frequent reports of their steadfastness and heroism and their generosity and humanity towards the Afghan population. All the same, there was still no realistic press account of the course of hostilities and the conditions under which the Soviet troops lived and fought, and no official casualty figures were revealed till after the decision to withdraw was announced. When Soviet conscripts who had served in Afghanistan were demobilised they often had difficulties with jobs, housing and medical care, and their efforts to secure redress were commonly met with indifference or hostility by the local authorities.[14] The attitude of the general public towards them was also at best ambivalent, and they often felt embittered by the contrast between what had been demanded of them and the cynical materialism and corruption of life back home. Small wonder that they tended to band together for mutual solace and protection, that they were sharply antagonistic towards the predominant semi-westernised youth culture, and that they sometimes formed themselves into vigilante groups that took the law into their own hands.[15]

Can the *afgantsy* be seen as a 'new force' in Soviet society, as some have suggested?[16] Surely not a major force, but one that could, perhaps, exert a significant political influence under certain circumstances. We cannot be sure in what direction that influence would point, or what circumstances would activate it. However, the sub-culture of the *afgantsy*, to judge by their reported behaviour and the songs that most clearly articulate their shared attitudes and values, is strong on mutual loyalty and comradeship, and on love of Russia, congenial to the firm hand but not to bureaucracy, has little time for liberal and intellectual niceties, is unimpressed by the West, and is marked by a rather crude romanticism that sometimes contains a distinct strain of the 'white man's burden'.[17] One thing is obvious: should Afghanistan come under the complete dominance of those at whose hands their comrades died, many of them would feel betrayed.

Now there is quite a lot in the sub-culture of the *afgantsy* that resonates with the views and attitudes found in the more radical Russian nationalist circles, like those of the *Pamiat'* Society. Up to now no organisational links have been reported, but a total triumph for the *Mujahideen* could provide the catalyst that would bring these two forces together and align them behind any possible challenge to Gorbachev's leadership.

The second factor I want to mention is the Islamic one, or to be more precise the political attitudes of the historically Muslim peoples of Soviet Central Asia. Two recent developments in this area are clearly worrying Moscow. One is the rise of ethnic nationalism, which these peoples share with those in other non-Russian areas such as the Baltic and the Caucasus. The second is a certain resurgence of Islamic belief and practice—how strong it is hard to estimate, but certainly enough to activate official counter-measures. As a Turkoman university lecturer recently wrote, 'In present circumstances the necessity of stepping up atheistic propaganda is becoming obvious',[18] and there is ample evidence that intensified anti-religious propaganda is being accompanied, as always, by intensified harassment of active Muslims by the police and local authorities.

The upsurge of local nationalism and of Islam would doubtless have occurred even without the massive purges that have recently swept the Central Asian republics, especially the largest ones, Uzbekistan and Kazakhstan; but the purges have clearly lent them greater force. A dramatic example is the rioting that occurred in Alma-Ata in 1986 when the Kazakh First Secretary Kunaev was replaced by the Russian Kolbin. The purges are seen as violating a kind of unwritten compact between Moscow and the Central Asians under which Moscow paid for their docility by tolerating high levels of corruption among the local elites, who in turn were indulgent to corrupt practices lower down the line, practices linked partly to traditional values and commitments.

The war in Afghanistan has thus been one among several factors currently tending to alienate the Central Asian peoples from the Soviet regime. It is obvious that the significance of the war has been quite different for them than for their Slavic fellow-citizens, given not only their Islamic background but also, in the case of the Tajiks, Uzbeks and Turkomen, a common ethnic identity with part of the population of Afghanistan. No romantic 'white man's burden' for their lads dying at the hands of the Afghan freedom-fighters!

It is difficult to judge how strong the linkage is between antagonism to the Afghanistan war and the ethnic, religious and socio-political grievances of Central Asians. There is certainly some direct evidence of such a linkage, especially in Tajikistan. Some time ago there were reports of mullahs who took advantage of the tolerance afforded them by officials and teachers in rural areas to publicly oppose the presence of Soviet troops in Afghanistan, on the grounds that they are being used to turn the Afghans into non-believers.[19] Even more dangerous forms of spillover have been alleged more recently. Vladimir Petkel, the (Russian) Chairman of the local KGB, told the Tajik Central Committee in December 1987 that radical Muslims and 'enemy agents' infiltrated over the border had been responsible for the big upsurge in draft-dodging and desertions from the Soviet armed forces, and that part of the Islamic clergy were calling for a 'holy war' against Soviet rule.[20] Such claims may or may not be exaggerated, but the Soviet authorities would not be drawing public attention to the linkage unless it was causing them major concern.

What, then, would be the effect in Central Asia of the establishment of an anti-communist Islamic regime in Kabul? To offer a confident answer to this question one would need far more knowledge of the area than I possess. However I would like to cite the opinion of the late Professor Alexandre Bennigsen, one of the leading authorities on Soviet Central Asia in the Western world. Speaking in an interview shortly before his death on 3 June 1988, Bennigsen said that the effect on Muslim society in Central Asia of a complete defeat for the Soviet Union would be 'colossal'. And he went on, 'It would be demonstrated that Soviet might was not invincible and that resistance is possible. What are the Afghans for Central Asia? It is a small, wild and poor country. So then, if the Afghans could inflict (such) a military and political defeat, then that makes anything possible. And everyone in Central Asia knows that. I think that in Soviet Russia they know it too.' Precisely for that reason, in Bennigsen's view, the Soviet leadership would not risk a complete withdrawal that would lead to a *Mujahideen* takeover, but would keep some troops in Kabul and in parts of the North.[21]

Bennigsen's estimate of the likely political impact in Soviet Central Asia of the loss of Afghanistan to anti-Soviet forces must be taken very seriously. Again, the significance of this for the USSR generally is likely to depend on the contingent circumstances. Taken in isolation, Moscow might well succeed in keeping the Central Asian population docile by a combination of political, economic and coercive measures. Even then, serious disorders in Central Asia could provoke ructions in the Soviet leadership. Should they occur simultaneously with nationalist outbreaks elsewhere in the USSR, or with worker unrest in Russia proper provoked by continued economic grievances, the consequences could be incalculable.

I started this chapter by arguing that the withdrawal from Afghanistan is unlikely to have deep-going and persistent domestic political implications in the USSR. However, as I have tried to show, it will certainly have some influence on a number of levels, and there are factors involved that, given a particularly unfavourable concatenation of circumstances, could have a major impact on the course of Soviet politics.

FOOTNOTES

1   See Bohdan Nahaylo, 'Ukrainian Mother's Protest attracts numerous Letters on the Afghanistan Theme', *Radio Liberty Research*, RL 188/87, 18 May 1987, and Sallie Wise, '"A War Should Never Have Happened": Soviet Citizens Assess the War in Afghanistan', *Radio Liberty Research*, RL 226/88, 1 June 1988.

2   The *Pamiat'* leader Dmitri Vasiliev is reportedly hostile to Russian involvement, and the nationalist writer Aleksandr Prokhanov, who sent many a gung-ho report from the battle-zones, now declares it to have been a 'mistake'. See *Literaturnaia gazeta*, 17 February 1988.

3   See William Zimmerman, *Soviet Perspectives on International Relations, 1956-67* (Princeton: Princeton University Press, 1969).

4   See Mark N. Katz, *The Third World in Soviet Military Thought* (Baltimore: The Johns Hopkins University Press, 1982); Stephen T. Hosner and Thomas W. Wolfe, *Soviet Policy and Practice Toward Third World Conflicts* (Lexington: Lexington Books, 1983); and S. Neil MacFarlane, *Superpower Rivalry and Third World Radicalism: The Idea of National Liberation* (London: Croom Helm, 1985).

5   See George W. Breslauer, 'Ideology and Learning in Soviet Third World Policy', *World Politics*, vol. 39, no. 3 (April 1987), pp.429-448, at pp.438-441.

6   Francis Fukuyama, 'Soviet Strategy in the Third World', in Andrzej Korbonski and Francis Fukuyama (eds.), *The Soviet Union and the Third World: The Last Three Decades* (Ithaca and London: Cornell University Press, 1987) pp.24-45.

7   See Jerry F. Hough, *The Struggle for the Third World: Soviet Debates and American Options* (Washington, D.C.: The Brookings Institution, 1986); and Elizabeth K. Valkenier, *The Soviet Union and the Third World: An Economic Bind* (New York: Praeger, 1983).

8   Oleg Bogomolov, 'Kto zhe oshibalsia?', *Literaturnaia gazeta*, 16 March 1988.

9   N. Simoniia, 'Chestno vesti nauchnuiu diskussiiu', *Aziia i Afrika segodnia*, no. 6, June 1988, p.17. I am indebted to Roderic Pitty for drawing my attention to this article.

10 'Afganistan—predvaritel'nye itogi', *Ogonek*, no. 30, 1988, p.25.

11 Daniel S. Papp, *Soviet Perceptions of the Developing World in the 1980's: The Ideological Basis* (Lexington: Lexington Books, 1985), p.136.

12 *Pravda,* 21 January 1988.

13 For example I. M. Dynin's collection *Zvezdy podviga: Na zemle Afganistana* (Moscow: Voennoe izdatel'stvo, 1985), which had a print run of 100,000.

14 There is now a campaign to enforce better treatment of Afghanistan veterans by local officials, but how far this will alleviate the widespread bitterness remains to be seen. See I. Ragimova, 'Pochet bez uvazheniia', *Bakinskii rabochii*, 8 July 1988; L. Belozerova, 'Vmesto serdtsa-kamennyi protez', *Pravda Ukrainy*, 10 July 1988; R. Ignatiev, 'S grifom "sekretno"', *Izvestiia*, 15 July 1988.

15 See Laura Tsagolova, in *Sobesednik* no. 1, January 1987; Savik Shuster, 'Problema afganiskikh veteranov v sovetskom obshchestve', *Radio Liberty Research*, RS 198/86, 9 December 1986.

16 'Soviet Veterans of the War in Afghanistan: a new Social Force?', *Radio Liberty Research*, RL 241/86, 24 June 1986.

17 See Valery Konovalov, 'Pesni veteranov Afganistana', *Radio Liberty Research*, RS 50/88, 6 June 1988; and the sources cited therein.

18 I. Akmuradov, 'V.I. Lenin o neobkhodimosti ideinoi bor'by s religiei', *Turkmenskaia Iskra*, 17 April 1988. See also Iu. Petrash, '"privychki" ostoiutsia navsegda?', *Sovetskaia Kirgiziia*, 14 May 1988; A. Alimov, 'Biznes na durmane', *Kommunist Tadzhikistana*, 13 May 1988.

19 See V. Rabiev, 'V klass...s koranom?' *Kommunist Tadzhikistana*, 31 January 1987.

20 *Kommunist Tadzhikistana*, 30 December 1987. Petkel also said that tens of clandestine Islamic leaders had been brought to trial in 1986-87.

21 'Pamiati A. Bennigsena (1913-1988)', *Radio Liberty Research*, RS 58/88, 5 July 1988, p.6.

6

The Soviet Armed Forces and the Afghan War

Geoffrey Jukes

Between the end of the Second World War in 1945 and the beginning of the intervention in Afghanistan in late 1979 the Soviet armed forces saw very little action compared to those of the USA, Britain and France, or even to those of smaller powers such as Israel, Egypt, Syria, Jordan, Iraq, Portugal, Australia and New Zealand outside the Communist world, and Vietnam within it. The use of overwhelming force ensured that in East Germany in 1953 and Hungary in 1956 violent resistance would be quickly suppressed, and that in Czechoslovakia in 1968 it would not be. attempted. Abstention from direct involvement in conflicts which they could not be sure of winning, such as Korea and Vietnam, helped the Soviet armed forces to acquire in the eyes of potential adversaries, and perhaps also in their own, a reputation for great capability, based on the one hand upon their undoubted achievements in the Second World War, and on the other upon their sheer size and estimates of the scale and quality of their equipment. So when Soviet forces entered Afghanistan, non-communist governments initially took their ability to dominate it for granted, and drew far-reaching strategic conclusions about Soviet designs on Gulf oil resources or sea-borne oil traffic. The

82

minority who decried these assessments, and argued that the intervention related solely to the Afghan internal situation, are probably justified by the outcome, because none of the dire prophecies was fulfilled. But there is a sense in which the argument cannot be resolved. The Soviet leaders could not demonstrate whether their objectives went beyond maintaining a Marxist regime in Kabul because the condition precedent was not achieved; their forces did not achieve the degree of control necessary to give them the choice.

It can, however, be inferred that their objectives were limited, because even after it became clear that no easy victory would be forthcoming they did not significantly increase the force, nor did they involve it on such a scale as to incur large casualties. Between 13000 and 15000 Soviet soldiers are estimated to have been killed in eight years, about a quarter of the 53000 Americans killed in an only slightly longer period in Vietnam. This is a grievous enough number for a country not officially at war, but for a force of about 115000 and a total armed force strength of several million a loss rate of 5 dead per day (little more than a quarter of the daily US loss rate in Vietnam) is militarily negligible (for comparison British losses in the brief Falklands War averaged 3.6 per day out of a force of only 6000); neither in the numbers nor in activity was the Soviet effort permitted to escalate as did the US effort in Vietnam. The Afghan Army was meant to, and did, bear the main burden of casualties throughout, with Soviet participation more dominant in aircraft, helicopter and artillery support, and in guarding of cities, roads or airfields than in infantry search-and-destroy operations, though they played a large part in those also.

That having been said, the Soviet military, exalted by its victorious traditions and NATO's flattering apprehensions, probably did not expect to stay so long and return with so little. The Soviet forces in Afghanistan repeated US experience in Vietnam, in that they did not lose, but could not win at a politically acceptable cost. There is a difference, in that the US withdrawal was mainly the result of internal opposition, whereas the Soviet decision to withdraw resulted mainly from an assessment that the damage caused by continued presence to Soviet relations with the West, China and the Third World outweighed any advantages it could confer; but the difference is of degree rather than kind, as foreign policy considerations were also factors in the US decision to leave Vietnam, and the involvement in Afghanistan was unpopular with the Soviet public.

The Changing Character of Warfare

Since the Second World War ended, the most common form of armed conflict has been warfare waged by insurrectionary forces within the bounds of a single country or colonial territory. These forces are for the most part lightly armed guerrillas, operating in relatively small groups against undefended or weakly defended targets of opportunity and, at least until the later stages of successful campaigns, avoiding contact with large conventional forces of the opposing government or colonial power. The strategy and tactics needed even for partial success against movements of this sort differ considerably from those needed in conventional warfare; the enemy usually holds the initiative, is hard to identify except when in action, heavy weapons such as tanks are of limited utility, and the principle of concentration of force has to be modified by the need to guard as many foreseeable targets as possible. Most actual fighting involves small groups, since guerrillas usually do not attack large ones; this places a larger premium than does conventional warfare on the individual skills and initiative of the private soldier and the lowest command levels, those of the section and platoon, and while seldom entailing a risk of resounding defeat also offers few chances of morale-boosting large-scale victories. In short, it has little in common with the kind of war conventional armed forces primarily exist to fight.

Several Western countries gained experience in fighting such wars both before and especially after 1945, and a body of analytical literature on counterinsurgency had come into existence which, if it did not prevent new mistakes being made, at least provided some chance of avoiding repetition of old ones; while the powers involved (chiefly France, the United Kingdom and the USA) made, for both geographical and historical reasons, considerable provision for 'distant limited war'. By contrast, the Soviet armed forces had fought no such wars since suppressing Ukrainian nationalist guerrillas in the late 1940s; and reluctance to refer even to the existence of anti-Soviet sentiments among the Soviet Union's second largest nationality ensured that that campaign engendered no body of analytical literature or practical training manuals on counterinsurgency.

In the early 1960s the policy-oriented *Voenno-istoricheskii zhurnal* published several articles on aspects of the Second World War which the Soviets had hitherto ignored, British Commando raids in Europe and American amphibious operations in the Pacific. The immediate consequence of this heightened interest in, by Soviet standards, small-unit warfare was the creation in 1963 of the Naval Infantry. There is no direct evidence whether this indicated a nascent interest in distant limited war or was merely intended to improve amphibious assault capacity for general war; if the former, the souring of the American experience in Vietnam may have weakened the case for Soviet pursuit of the expensive distant limited war option, but the subsequent development, exercise and deployment patterns of the force tend to suggest that improvement of general war capability was what was intended—in the Indo-Pacific area, at least, the Naval Infantry protects naval facilities and practises opposed landings on islands close to Soviet coasts and to Japan; it does not generally accompany Soviet out-of-area naval visits to foreign countries, and in its twenty-five years of existence has not been employed even symbolically either to support or to intimidate a Third World government. It does not, therefore, appear to constitute a departure from the Soviet armed forces' concentration, in doctrine, training and procurement, on preparation for winning, or more precisely, not losing, in 'Big War' against the US alliance system.

The Soviet armed forces had not stood totally aside from study of insurgency or counterinsurgency, but the pattern of their involvement was mostly indirect and politically determined. Weapons and in some cases advisers were sent to insurgents such as the MPLA in pre-independence Angola or the North in pre-unification Vietnam, or to governments faced with internal insurgency, such as the MPLA in post-independence Angola or the Dergue in post-1974 Ethiopia—but Soviet combat forces were not; where needed, as in Angola, they were supplied by others, notably Cuba.

This policy is usually described as surrogacy, and when examined at all tends to be explained as expansionism by stealth, aimed at achieving increased strength or influence while avoiding a direct confrontation with the United States. The assiduousness with which the Soviet Union has abstained from direct participation in Third World conflicts would seem to require more specific explanation than this, or than the self-serving Soviet explanation that the Soviet Union, being anti-imperialist, has an obligation to assist anti-imperialist Third World governments or movements, but no requirement to fight colonial-type wars itself. For present purposes, however, it is less necessary to seek an explanation for this Soviet behaviour than to note that because of it the Soviet forces which entered Afghanistan in the closing days of 1979 lacked not only experience in counterinsurgency, but also other prerequisites, from a doctrine for sub-conventional war down to training manuals for small-unit actions. They were forces trained and configured for 'Big War', organised as an Army (40th), and initially including even air defence missile troops, though the *Mujahideen* had no aircraft; and when it proved more difficult than was probably expected to cope with the Afghan resistance, not only was there no significant increase in the size of the force, though its quality improved over time, there was no indication of a particularly high degree of professional interest in the war, even though it was the first prolonged campaign involving substantial numbers of Soviet troops to have been undertaken since 1945.

Soviet Analysis of the Afghan War

Official statements or General Staff documents which might explain this apparent professional insouciance are not available, so analysis has to depend on the mostly negative evidence of the military press, particularly the daily newspaper *Krasnaia zvezda* and the fortnightly journal *Kommunist vooruzhennykh sil.*

Neither of these is a purely military journal. Although the mast-head of *Krasnaia zvezda* proclaims it to be the 'Central Organ of the Ministry of Defence', and that of *Kommunist vooruzhennykh sil* describes it as the 'Military-Political Journal of the Main Political Directorate of the Soviet Army and Navy', both are published and printed at the same address, both are under strong political control, and the Main Political Directorate is the organ through which 'the Central Committee of the CPSU exercises leadership of Party-political work ... and ensures Party influence on all sides of the life and activity of the forces'.[1] The newspaper is aimed at the troops in general, whereas the magazine is intended, as its name suggests, for Party members in the Armed Forces, and especially for the Political Officers: much of its content in fact consists of articles and lecture notes to be used by these officers in carrying out their duties; and since those duties[2] involve not merely political indoctrination but a substantial role in raising unit efficiency and sustaining morale, any military policy issue of general importance is soon reflected in its contents; in a society which from its earliest days has required its military to exhibit political commitment as well as (and sometimes ahead of) professional competence, the avowedly political purposes of the two journals make them more rather than less reliable guides to the role the Afghanistan experience is accorded at the highest level, where military and political attitudes mesh most closely.

Examination of the issues of both publications from the beginning of 1980 (that is, a few days after Soviet troops entered Afghanistan) to the end of June 1988, suggests either a politically-decreed conspiracy of silence or a relative military lack of interest, or both, until well into 1986. *Krasnaia zvezda* published only a handful of articles each year about the war, mostly of the 'hearts and minds' variety, and concerns known to be arising in the public attitude to the war were reflected only indirectly, the first and most important of these turning out to be not military but racial.

The original intervention force had included large numbers of Central Asian troops of similar ethnicity to large minorities of the Afghan population (Uzbek, Kirghiz, Tajik and Turkmen), and when many of these troops were withdrawn in March 1980 there were widespread rumours that they had proved unreliable. The explanation was in fact more mundane; for security and administrative reasons the original intervention was conducted by forces of the Turkestan Military District, which borders on Afghanistan, and as few of its units are maintained at full strength in peacetime, numbers of local reservists were called up; inevitably most of these were Central Asians, predominantly Uzbeks. A reservist's liability to recall in peacetime is limited to ninety days,[3] so they were released by the end of March 1980, and replaced by active-service conscripts. But the rumours of unreliability or disaffection continued, because they reflect a Russian attitude to Central Asians which has deep historical roots, going back to the period of Muslim overlordship of the medieval Russian city-states (the so-called 'Tartar yoke') and subsequent Russian advances at the expense of the former Islamic conquerors. Until 1916 Muslims were not regarded as sufficiently reliable to be accepted into the Russian Army, and when the large losses of 1914-15 caused the Empire to declare them liable for non-combatant service widespread Muslim riots had to be forcibly suppressed. And although in the Second World War most Central Asian soldiers held to their allegiance, the Germans were able to recruit relatively large numbers of Muslim prisoners-of-war into anti-Soviet units.[4] The long-standing Russian distrust of Central Asians is compounded within the armed forces by two other factors: first, the relatively lower educational levels of Central Asians mean that proportionately fewer of them are found suitable for the more technical arms of service, or for commissioning as officers, and second, their often poor knowledge of Russian makes them less desired in combat units, where quick response to oral orders may be vital. They therefore tend to cluster in the lower ranks and the less technical non-combat arms such as construction units, giving rise on the one hand to Russian allegations of 'dodging the column', and on the other to claims by Central Asian Muslims of discrimination against them.[5] In respect to Afghanistan in particular a widespread attitude among Russians was one of resentment that Central Asians were allegedly not pulling their weight in an essentially Central Asian dispute, while young Russians were being killed in their stead.

The response of *Krasnaia zvezda* was to ensure that from 1981 onwards virtually every published photograph of Soviet troops in Afghanistan included at least one identifiable Muslim, and every article made some mention of one. In one case, an article devoted to a captain commanding an infantry battalion, a dual purpose was served, showing Central Asian soldiers that Muslims could command Russians, and showing Russians that not all Muslims were unpromotable non-combatants.[6] Nevertheless the total number of articles on Afghanistan remained low.

Kommunist vooruzhennykh sil accorded the war an even lower profile; no article specifically devoted to it appeared until the very end of 1984,[7] and such passing references as there were related to its political rather than military nature.[8] What this meant in practice was that the formal political instruction given to troops not serving in Afghanistan (around 97.2% of them) would for the first five years of the involvement have included no references to it, because the journal, intended as the unit Political Officers' 'Bible', gave them no guidance on what to say.

This does not, of course, mean that the experience gained in the Soviet armed forces' first prolonged major campaign in forty years was receiving no professional evaluation—for it not to do so would be a total breach with standard practice within the profession of arms, and operational problems were numerous; they certainly included the organisational difficulties of reorienting a large-unit army to small-unit warfare, equipment difficulties ranging from the need to provide more and better radios for command and control of a force fragmented into large numbers of small detachments, to the necessity to find countermeasures against the very effective Stinger anti-aircraft missiles supplied to the *Mujahideen*, training for mountain warfare of young Russians, most of whom had never seen a mountain before, and all of whom had basically been trained to fight mainly from vehicles rather than on foot. These problems must have been considered, but there was clearly no feeling that any conclusions reached were important enough to require generalisation and broad diffusion to the armed forces as a whole. In *Kommunist vooruzhennykh sil* this relative indifference continued until the middle of 1986; on average references to Afghanistan appeared in only about one issue in four, and were mostly incidental or anecdotal.

A radical change took place from July 1986, after which date about three issues in every four contained some mention of the Afghanistan commitment. Initially the most frequent theme was mention of meetings in various Military Districts at which officers with experience in Afghanistan discussed its relevance and how to diffuse it to others. A possible pointer to the future is that foremost among these[9] was the Far Eastern Military District. The area in which it would operate in war includes much mountainous terrain, but so do several other Military Districts (for example the Carpathian, Transcaucasus, Turkestan and Central Asian) which did not show the same degree of interest.[10] The Far Eastern Military District was then commanded by Army General D.T. Iazov, who at the end of the year was transferred to Moscow as Deputy Defence Minister for Cadres and in May

1987 abruptly promoted to Minister of Defence over the heads of many who were senior to him, including four Marshals. That the experience of the troops in Afghanistan began to be widely diffused only in the seventh year of the intervention strongly suggests that senior military opinion regarded it as of little relevance to their perceived main function, the successful conduct of 'Big War' against high-technology adversaries. That the first commander to take it up became Minister of Defence within a year of doing so probably means little; when Iazov brought up the issue in mid-1986 he can have had little or no inkling of the rapid promotion which was soon to come his way, and which appears to have resulted from the impression he made during Gorbachev's visit to Vladivostok in July of that year. In his previous command, the Central Asian Military District, he would have been well-informed about operations in Afghanistan, responsibility for which centred on the adjacent Turkestan Military District, and since the Far Eastern Military District in the event of war would have to advance through similarly mountainous terrain in North-East China, against an enemy both less well-equipped and more guerrilla-oriented than the NATO countries, it would not be surprising that its commander was early in seeking to generalise the Afghanistan experience once it had been made clear (by means and for reasons as yet unknown) that the previous apparent indifference to it had been abandoned. In short, it is likely that Iazov's initiative in promoting discussion of sub-conventional war and his later elevation were both resultants of an efficiency for which he had previously been noted,[11] rather than that the one led to the other. This interpretation tends to be supported by the fact that his elevation to Minister had not, at least up to the end of his first year in office, resulted in any indications of increased importance being attached to the Afghanistan experience.

In *Krasnaia zvezda* photographs of and articles about Afghanistan, ranging between three and five a month up to the second quarter of 1985, approximately doubled during the second half of 1986, and by early 1988 were appearing almost daily. Like the references in *Kommunist vooruzhennykh sil* they were largely of the 'Hearts and Minds' variety, stressing the humanitarian aspect of the intervention; descriptions of fighting usually related to operations undertaken jointly with or in support of the Afghan Army, and where they concerned Soviet troops

90

alone were normally accounts of small-unit actions, casting Soviet forces in a benign light, for example by narratives about attacks on columns taking food to Afghan villages which had been isolated by *Mujahideen* mining of roads. Their emphasis on Afghan participation and their tendency not to refer to large-scale Soviet actions were probably intended to counter suggestions (almost universal where two armies fight together) that Soviet troops were taking more than their fair share of the burden. But they also reflect reality, which is that the Soviet role has been mainly one of support, that most of the ground force effort has been devoted to garrison duty in main cities, keeping open the roads between them and, especially, the main road from the Soviet border to Kabul, and that there have been few large-scale pitched battles because guerrilla forces in Afghanistan, as elsewhere, prefer to avoid them, and are difficult to trap into them because of their superior local knowledge and ability to merge into the civilian population.

Experience of sub-conventional warfare probably brought most line infantry units to a reasonable level of competence as time went on, but increasing mention in connection with Afghanistan of the Soviet Army formations most trained for small-unit work, the Airborne Forces (*Vozdushno-desantnye voiska*, or VDV), began to be observed from early 1985.[12] This may have resulted from perceived inadequacy in performance by the ordinary motorised infantry units, but equally could have arisen from a desire to provide these elite units with experience particularly suited to their training, their equipment and the aptitudes they are required to develop; they are the world's largest airborne force (there are eight divisions of them), they had been present in limited numbers since 1981, there were no disasters to motorised infantry units sufficient to make their replacement by 'better' troops a matter of urgency, and the level of Soviet activity did not rise significantly as a consequence of increased VDV presence.

Although the Soviet media had for long made occasional references to the Afghan-Pakistani discussions about a political settlement, the Soviet Politburo's decision to withdraw from Afghanistan initially appears to have caught the military-political apparatus somewhat by surprise; the first article on the progress of 'national reconciliation' appeared in the same issue of *Kommunist vooruzhennykh sil* as one devoted to improving combat cooperation between Soviet and Afghan forces,[13] and two months later the journal reported that an 'Internationalist' club had been formed in Krasnodar for the purpose of enabling Afghanistan veterans to pass on their experience to youth about to be called up,[14] both references implying that substantial presence was to be sustained for some time to come. Bearing in mind that the journal exists mainly to provide Party members and Political officers with justifications for Party policy, it appears to have been somewhat dilatory in adjusting to imminent withdrawal. Issue number 15 for 1987 (cleared for publication in mid-July, and published early in August) contained no more than a passing reference to the Afghan Armed Forces as 'an effective weapon for reconciliation',[15] and six weeks passed before publication of a full-scale article, which claimed that reconciliation was succeeding, but pointed to a number of obstacles still to be overcome, presenting an overall picture of heavily qualified optimism.[16] The likely future of post-withdrawal Afghanistan received no further mention until early 1988, when another article by the same author appeared. Contrary to previous Soviet writings, which tended to depict the *Mujahideen* as hired bandits with little or no popular support, he made the very significant admission that about half the population of the country had been 'drawn into the orbit of the counterrevolution', but assured readers of the high regard in which the Soviet forces were held, and referred to their success, jointly with the Afghan Army, in raising the siege of Khost in December 1987. As to the future, while casting doubts on US willingness to cease intervening, he said no more than that attitudes to reconciliation showed who were the Afghans' true friends,[17] and avoided even implying that continued outside intervention might cause a slowing-down in the pace of the Soviet withdrawal. In short, he conveyed a message that the Afghan episode was over as far as the Soviet armed forces were concerned, and that it carried no implications for the future conduct of warfare.

The message can also, of course, be taken as a military attempt to put a bold face on failure by depicting the entire episode as of no consequence. This interpretation, however, would be tenable only in the presence of evidence that at an earlier stage the military attached high professional importance to it, and, as already indicated, the available evidence suggests that they did not.

The modesty of the military investment in Afghanistan contrasts with the high investment of Soviet political prestige there, the mere fact of intervention implying a political belief that winning was possible. There is no plausible evidence on how the military leadership reacted when the idea of intervention was first mooted; it is simply not known whether it responded enthusiastically to a chance, agreed reluctantly to what it saw as a distraction from its 'real' purpose, or simply did what it was told with no particular feeling either way. In addition to factors already mentioned—the relative smallness of the force, the refusal to increase it, and its fairly low casualty rate—its position in the hierarchical structure of military command has also been low. While very high-ranking officers have visited Afghanistan to advise, consult, exhort and pressurise, the 'Limited Contingent' has been administratively considered an 'Army', corresponding in size to a Western 'corps', and commanded by a Lieutenant-General, which in the Soviet armed forces is a two-star rank, broadly equivalent to a Major-General in the US, British or Australian Armies.[18] The status of the force is therefore lower than that of Military Districts within the Soviet Union or Groups of Forces outside it (in Poland, East Germany, Czechoslovakia and Hungary) most of which are commanded by a (three-star) Colonel-General or (four-star) Army General. It is probable that the force in Afghanistan was subordinate to the adjacent Turkestan Military District[19] through which its needs were met, and it may be either a sign of satisfaction with overall performance, or at least of a wish to demonstrate satisfaction, that in 1988, with the withdrawal impending, Colonel-General N.I. Popov, who has commanded the Turkestan Military District since 1982, was promoted to Army General. This rank can be conferred only by the Presidium of the Supreme Soviet,[20] which in practice means by the Party leadership.

The present commander of 40th Army, Lieutenant-General B.V. Gromov, gave a press conference in Kabul on 14 May 1988, the day before the Geneva agreements came into effect.[21] He denied that any Soviet unit, however small, had ever retreated before the *Mujahideen* and asserted that there could therefore be 'no question of any military defeat'. The withdrawal was 'not a retreat', but 'the completion of an internationalist mission' and 'fulfilment of the Geneva agreements', undertaken because 'so it seems, this step will serve to create an

93

atmosphere of trust, necessary to Soviet-American relations'; Gromov thereby defended his troops' performance, acknowledged subordination of the local and purely military considerations to the global and political, and hinted at scepticism as to whether the withdrawal will serve its intended purpose.

His chief political officer, Major-General A. Zakharov, wrote in *Krasnaia zvezda* a week later,[22] praising the conduct of Soviet troops, expressing a high opinion of the Afghan Army, and claiming considerable evidence of the respect Soviet society held for those who fought in Afghanistan; but he cited an instance of official neglect to house a wounded returnee, and admitted that such cases were not infrequent. His assessment of what had been achieved was mostly vague and impressionistic; the only figures he cited were for repair, construction and electrification work done by troops, medical treatment provided to civilians by military doctors, and supplies distributed to the civilian population

There is evidence, mostly from diplomatic sources in Kabul, of social problems among the Soviet troops, centering around drug-taking and black market activities. These are similar in nature to problems which arose among US troops in Vietnam, but lesser in scale because of the smaller size of the force, the low pay of Soviet conscripts and the tight restrictions on their free time. Despite the care taken by the leadership to project a public image of gratitude to the troops, there have been indications that some returnees are disillusioned by public and official indifference. At a 'Round Table' discussion of the history and development of the armed forces, arranged by the Party journal *Kommunist* and by *Kommunist vooruzhennykh sil*, S. Epifantsev, a Secretary of the Central Committee of the Communist Youth League, raised the question of 'why some of the young lads who were given awards for their feats in Afghanistan don't wear the medals they won with honour? It is because the medals they received are not just a reward, they are a symbol and sign that society cares. When this care and concern aren't shown in anything else except the medal, the lads begin to doubt'.[23] In the absence of data there is no way to assess the magnitude of this problem, or the extent to which service in Afghanistan has aggravated difficulties of readjustment beyond those some other ex-conscripts experience on return to civilian life. It is *prima facie* unlikely to bulk as large in Soviet society as it did in the USA, because the numbers involved are much smaller and conscription is an accepted fact of life, whereas in the USA and Australia it was reintroduced specifically for the Vietnam War and was therefore politically controversial in itself. Furthermore, the low level of publicity accorded the war by the government-controlled media prevented its becoming a major focus of public discontent, and by the time a protest movement might have developed, the need for it had been pre-empted by the decision to withdraw in relatively short order.

Soviet Re-evaluation of the Military

Overarching all the specific reasons why the Afghanistan experience has had less effect than might have been expected on the Soviet armed forces are general considerations which derive from *perestroika* and *glasnost'*. Under these rubrics the armed forces are experiencing criticism to an extent hitherto unknown for glossing over failures of the past, in particular the disasters of the early months of the Second World War, and for poor discipline, bad interpersonal relations and over-preoccupation with presenting an 'image' in the present.[24] These criticisms are, however, part of a general process of re-evaluation going on in Soviet society, and not a specific consequence of performance in Afghanistan.

In the military sphere the re-evaluation is the most comprehensive to have been undertaken since the early 1960s. So far it is mostly conceptual, for the simple reason that a change in ideas on war necessarily precedes by several years any consequential changes in the size, training and equipment of the armed forces. This is particularly the case where equipment is concerned, because a weapons system commonly takes a decade to develop and is then in service for two decades or more.

It is, however, already clear from numerous statements and articles by political leaders that the re-evaluation began soon after Gorbachev came to power, and was essentially complete by the middle of 1987.[25] Its main features are a shift from deterrence of war by appearing too strong to be defeated, to deterrence by ability to inflict unacceptable damage on an aggressor in any conceivable circumstances. The shift is mainly one of emphasis, because neither superpower has ever placed all

95

its strategic eggs into a single basket; the United States since 1945 and the Soviet Union since 1957 have each relied for deterrence of all-out war on the ability to devastate the other's homeland, whichever attacks first, and for deterrence of lesser threats on the maintenance of conventional forces large enough at best to appear capable of winning without escalation to nuclear war, and at worst to enforce a 'pause' on an aggressor, forcing him to choose between desisting and escalating to nuclear war. But the balance to be maintained between the two capabilities has been the most fruitful cause of friction between the United States and its allies; if it has not caused equal overt dissension within the Soviet alliance system, this is mainly because that system adds far less to Soviet strength, containing no major second-rank powers comparable to West Germany, France, the United Kingdom or Japan. Within the Soviet military establishment it was the subject of considerable debate between 1955 and 1965,[26] and was resolved by adoption under Brezhnev of a 'two-track' solution, involving very large increases in nuclear forces and upgrading, including in some cases numerical increases, of conventional forces. The pursuit of this costly solution has contributed to the Soviet Union's present economic problems, and also tended not only to provoke countervailing increases in defence spending by the US and allies, but to isolate the Soviet Union politically. The outcome was increased expenditure without increased security, and Gorbachev has indicated awareness of this on a number of occasions, though usually in general terms rather than in a specifically Soviet context.[27] At the 19th Party Conference in June 1988 his speech included a statement that henceforward improvement of defence capacity would have to be in qualitative rather than quantitative parameters, and this oblique indication of possible cuts in size and cost was made somewhat more specific by Iazov on 9 August in *Krasnaia zvezda*, where he wrote of the need to restructure the forces in such a way that they would remain effective at any conceivable level of reduction.

Conclusion

Overall, therefore, the Soviet military appears to have regarded the Afghanistan experience less seriously than might have been expected. The commitment never escalated significantly beyond its original level, nor was there any apparent intention to take over the major combat role from the numerically smaller and less well-equipped Afghan Army. The decision to withdraw was not prompted by military necessity, but the decision to leave rather than to seek victory by increased involvement probably derived not only from assessment of the harm the presence was creating to specific and current relationships with particular countries, but to Gorbachev's frequently-stated general disbelief in the feasibility of military solutions to political problems.[28]

Not to be disregarded also is the relative unimportance of Afghanistan. The 'Great Game' of the nineteenth century arose not from any estimate that Afghanistan would be a valuable acquisition, but from mutual fear; on the one hand, British suspicions of a southward Russian drive towards India and on the other Russian apprehensions of British designs on Central Asia. Both participants made military forays into Afghanistan, but with forces never exceeding a few thousand troops, and both eventually agreed to regard it as a buffer zone between their respective possessions, not merely because of the tenacity with which the inhabitants defended their independence, but also because it offered little recompense for the effort that conquest would require. The ending of British rule in the subcontinent removed Soviet cause for concern, provided that US influence did not replace British; in the case of Pakistan it did, but as long as Pakistani-Afghan relations remained bad, which they were more often than not, there was no prospect of US influence advancing to the Soviet southern borders via Afghanistan. US alliance-building in the area concentrated upon Iran and Pakistan, and it was therefore relatively easy for the Soviets from the mid-1950s onwards to establish a position of strong influence in Afghanistan, without any major competition from the Western powers; well before the overthrow of the monarchy in 1973 the Soviet Union had become the main supplier of economic and military aid, and the largest trading partner.

In summary it was demonstrated that virtually any regime in Kabul would consider it advantageous to seek a satisfactory relationship with the Soviet Union, and from that angle the seizure of power by the Afghan Communists in April 1978 was an unneeded complication. It created a regime whose fate the Soviet Union could not regard with indifference, as it could hitherto; and when that regime in turn became unstable the attempt to sustain it by direct military intervention created for the Soviets not only world-wide political problems, but specifically regional military difficulties. The arguments for withdrawal eventually came to outweigh those for staying, but as in the case of the decision to intervene, there is no evidence about the military inputs to the discussion which resulted in the decision to leave. It must be assumed that their advice was sought on at least the basic question 'Will Soviet strategic interests be harmed by withdrawal?' The evidence already adduced, indicating that the level of professional interest was low throughout, tends to suggest that their answer amounted to 'No', and that most or all of them welcome the removal of a commitment which conflicts both with the armed forces' perceived and proclaimed primary mission and with the need to restructure the forces towards greater efficiency and economy. The annihilation of General Elphinstone's force in Afghanistan in 1841 had no great consequences for the British military, and there is no reason to believe that the Soviet experience (which included no comparable defeat) will have any greater impact; a trend towards avoidance of involvement in regional conflicts will probably have been given greater impetus by the lack of success in Afghanistan, but the trend is motivated by politics and economics rather than by strategy, and the withdrawal is merely one of its manifestations.

FOOTNOTES

1 *Voennyi Entsiklopedicheskii Slovar'* (Moscow: Voenizdat, 1983) p.195.
2 For example, the then Defence Minister described Party-political work as a factor which 'multiplies the morale and combat qualities of the officers and men', and the military press as serving as 'an all-army rostrum for propagating advanced experience in training and education of servicemen': Marshal A.A. Grechko, *The Armed Forces of the Soviet Union* (Moscow: Progress Publishers, 1972) pp.289 and 314.
3 'Zakon SSSR o vseobshchei voinskoi obiazannosti', in *Svod Zakonov SSSR* (Moscow: Izvestiia, 1982) vol.9, pp.181-202.
4 The Germans formed armies or 'Legions' from prisoners of Russian, Ukrainian, Cossack, Caucasus and Central Asian ethnicities: *Signal-Dokumentation* (Hamburg: Jahr-Verlag KG, 1977) vol.4, pp.128-137. Relative to their numbers the Central Asians provided the most volunteers

(the Turkestan and Azerbaijan Legions), and were employed in action more than the others.

5   For example, Brezhnev, in dedicating the memorial complex at Stalingrad, listed Central Asians last among the defenders, though their numbers must have greatly exceeded those of Balts, who were listed well ahead of them: *Kommunist vooruzhennykh sil*, no.5, 1980, p.33.

6   Subsequently this officer, Ruslan Sultanovich Aushev, was author of an article on command and tactics, *Kommunist vooruzhennykh sil*, no.2, 1986, pp.45-50. By then he was a Major, and a passing reference to him in *Kommunist vooruzhennykh sil*, no. 24, 1987, p.70, indicated that by the end of 1987 he had been promoted again, to Lieutenant-Colonel. He was featured yet again in *Kommunist vooruzhennykh sil*, no.16, 1988, pp.69-70; that Central Asian officers are hard to find is illustrated by the fact that although a Muslim he is not a Central Asian but an Ingush from the Caucasus.

7   Colonel A. Khorunzhii, 'Afganistan: v boiakh za revoliutsiiu', *Kommunist vooruzhennykh sil*, no.24, 1984, pp.76-79.

8   For example, Captain 1st Rank N. Minaev, 'Internatsional'nyi kharakter zashchity zavoevanii sotsializma', *Kommunist vooruzhennykh sil*, no.11, 1984, pp.72-78, lists it on p.76 as one of a series of acts which also includes provision of support in various wars and crises to North Korea, East Germany, Cuba and Vietnam, as well as the invasions of Hungary and Czechoslovakia.

9   In *Kommunist vooruzhennykh sil*, nos.17, 1986, p.92, and 18, 1986, p.95.

10 The Commander of the Turkestan Military District, Colonel-General Popov, first referred publicly to the need to make more use of Afghanistan experience in an article published in November 1987(*Kommunist vooruzhennykh sil*, no.22, 1987, p.68), fourteen months after meetings in the Far Eastern Military District.

11 An article by Colonel G. Kashuba refers to his manifestation of this quality when commanding a Division in the Transbaikal Military District as long ago as 1967-70: *Krasnaia zvezda*, 13 April 1985, p.3.

12 For example, in *Kommunist vooruzhennykh sil*, nos.4, 1985, pp 59-64; 13, 1985, p.44; 1, 1987, pp.31-35; and 10, 1987, pp.53-57. Frequent front-page photographs in *Krasnaia zvezda* showed VDV soldiers, not described as such but identifiable by details of their uniforms. In mid-May 1988, VDV troops were prominent in Soviet television pictures of the first withdrawals.

13 Colonel N. Vasil'iev, 'Po zakonam bratstva', *Kommunist vooruzhennykh sil*, no.10, 1987, pp.53-57, and Major A. Oliinik, 'Vesna trevog i nadezhd', *Kommunist vooruzhennykh sil*, no.10, 1987, pp.87-91.

14 *Kommunist vooruzhennykh sil*, no.14, 1987, p.93.

15 *Kommunist vooruzhennykh sil*, no.15, 1987, p.89.

16 Captain A. Mel'nik, 'Trudnye shagi k miru', *Kommunist vooruzhennykh sil*, no.18, 1987, pp.80-82.

17 *Kommunist vooruzhennykh sil*, no.2, 1988, pp.83-86.

18 For comparison, US commanders in Korea and Vietnam were of five and four-star ranks, and the United Kingdom task force in the Falklands War was commanded by a four-star Admiral.

19 The subsequent postings of two of the Afghanistan force commanders confirm that it ranks below a Military District. One became First Deputy Commander of the Carpathian Military District, the other Commander of the Transcaucasus Military District.

20 *Voennyi Entsiklopedicheskii Slovar'* (Moscow: Voenizdat, 1983) p.273.

21 *Krasnaia zvezda*, 15 May 1988, p.1.

22 *Krasnaia zvezda*, 21 May 1988, p.3.

23 *Kommunist vooruzhennykh sil*, no.4, 1988, p.25.

24 These and other criticisms are presented and discussed at length in a round table discussion in *Kommunist vooruzhennykh sil*, no.4, 1988, pp.9-26.

25 During his visit to the United States in August 1988 the Chief of the Soviet General Staff, Marshal Akhromeev, told his hosts that the evaluation had taken two years and been completed in mid-1987.

26 This debate was analysed at the time in a number of Western writings, including Raymond L. Garthoff, *The Soviet Image of Future War* (Washington: Public Affairs Press, 1959); H.S. Dinerstein, *War and the Soviet Union* (New York: Praeger, 1959 and 1964) and Malcolm Mackintosh, *Juggernaut* (London: Secker and Warburg, 1967).

27 For example, in his 25 February 1986 *Political Report of the Central Committee to the 27th Party Congress of the CPSU* (Moscow: Novosti Press Agency, 1986), he said at p.81 that present levels of nuclear weapons were much too high and ensured 'equal danger', whereas 'genuine equal security is ensured not by the highest possible but by the lowest possible level of strategic parity'.

28 For example, in his book *Perestroika: New Thinking for Our Country and the World* (London: Collins, 1987) pp.188-189 and 219-220.

7

Afghanistan and Soviet Alliances

Robert F. Miller

In contrast to the aftermath of the US withdrawal from Vietnam, which evoked a wave of speculation in both the US and its associated countries about an allegedly inevitable collapse of the global American alliance system, the pre- and post-Geneva period of the Afghanistan negotiations have seen a paucity of such speculation in the media of the countries that are the subject of this chapter. Direct consideration of the implications of the withdrawal has apparently been a *taboo* topic for the Soviet media and, evidently, for the media of its alliance partners as well, although there have been nuances of difference, as we shall see later on.

The approach of this chapter is first to present certain background factors of a theoretical and contextual nature; next, to distinguish among the various classes of Soviet alliance partners; and finally to look at the differential impact that the Soviet withdrawal from Afghanistan may have on the respective types of allies. Gorbachev's 'new political thinking' is presumably informed by a general desire to 'wipe the slate clean' in dealing with the outside world so as to maximise opportunities to pursue a more cost-effective set of policies at home and abroad in keeping with his perceptions of the structure and behaviour appropriate for a modern superpower in the age of the 'scientific

101

and technical revolution'.[1] Bringing that desire to fruition is not an easy task, however, because of the structures, commitments and ideological presuppositions relating to Soviet foreign policy in general and the Soviet alliance system in particular which Gorbachev has inherited from his predecessors. Not even Gorbachev himself can be considered an entirely free agent in such matters. Although less rigid than his predecessors, and evidently most of his colleagues as well, Gorbachev, too, is inevitably a product of the system which nurtured him and elevated him to its pinnacle of power. The process of dismantling the inhibiting conceptions and the edifice of ideological rationale behind the Soviet alliance system to make shifts like the withdrawal from Afghanistan possible has occupied a good deal of the attention of Gorbachev's foreign policy advisers and other would-be 'influentials' for several years.

The Nature of Soviet Alliances

Problems of dealing with allies were almost as difficult as those of dealing with enemies for the fledgling post-Revolutionary Soviet state. On the one, hand, there was an expectation that a successful World Revolution would eliminate the major antagonisms of international relations; the victorious socialist countries would form a single world polity, conceived of as a federation of Soviet republics (in the context of the Russo-Polish War and the recent abortive Soviet republics set up in Hungary and Bavaria). The organisation of the Communist International, or Comintern, reflected this conception, the individual constituent parties being formally considered national sections of a single world revolutionary body, headquartered ('temporarily') in Moscow, but headed by an executive comprising representatives of foreign communist parties as well as the All-Union Communist Party (Bolshevik). In fact, of course, the Comintern was soon 'Bolshevised', that is, subordinated to the national interests of the USSR as interpreted by Stalin. On the other hand, the opportunities for strategic and tactical agreements with individual states of the capitalist world, predicted by Lenin in his famous treatise *Imperialism: the Highest Stage of Capitalism*, made it incumbent on Soviet rulers to seek out alliances even among the 'subjectively' most anti-Bolshevik national elites in order to break the 'hostile capitalist encirclement'.

The attitude toward communist party-ruled states as somehow legitimately part of the Soviet 'patrimony' by virtue of Moscow's leadership of international socialism in the on-going struggle for survival and eventual supremacy *vis-à-vis* international capitalism has persisted in recognisable form to the present day. The Brezhnev Doctrine, enunciated in the wake of the Soviet-led Warsaw Pact invasion of Czechoslovakia in 1968, was its most brazen expression in recent years. Under its terms, those socialist states within Moscow's security grasp are required to limit their aspirations for domestic and foreign policy autonomy in the name of socialist unity and the broader interests of socialism as defined by Soviet leaders, when and if they choose to make such a determination. In his quest for new models and methods to make socialism economically more efficient and politically more attractive, Gorbachev has tacitly conceded much of the freedom of domestic manoeuvre previously sought by the East Europeans, but he has pointedly not specifically repudiated the doctrine of 'limited sovereignty'. Indeed, in his book, *Perestroika,* he re-emphasises the need for all of the COMECON states, at least, to 'coordinate' their policies and to take both 'their own and common interests' into account in fashioning their domestic and foreign policies.[2] It is clearly premature to assert that the Brezhnev Doctrine is no longer operative.

In contrast to the communist party-ruled states, for which a kind of mutual obligation attaches, Soviet alliances with non-communist states are regarded as a much less binding type of encumbrance. The Ribbentrop-Molotov Agreement and the various other interwar treaties with the Baltic Republics, Poland and Romania, to name only a few, demonstrated that Soviet behaviour toward 'infidel' powers could be amazingly cynical and Machiavellian. Soviet security interests, commonly enunciated for the 'faithful' in terms of the dialectics of the 'international class struggle', overrode any consideration of mutual obligations with such partners. If the latter were strong enough to maintain Soviet interest in fulfilment, then useful treaties and alliances could be undertaken, but the Soviets clearly had no sense of moral commitment to alliance partners that were 'objectively' ideologically hostile or neutral. Other powers behave this way, too, but the Soviets have often seemed unusually opportunistic in their attitudes to one-time friends and allies, even by the prevailing low world standards.

From this brief resumé of the nature of Soviet alliances it is clear that there is a substantial difference between the treatment the Soviets accord to communist party-ruled states and to those without such a pedigree. As we shall see, there are degrees of difference even within these two categories and in the states lying within a third, nominally 'transitional', category.

The Varieties of Soviet Alliances

The decision to withdraw from Afghanistan does, indeed, represent a significant departure from Soviet policy toward countries allied with the USSR. It could have implications even for Moscow's allies in 'the socialist world', as Gorbachev now calls countries where communist parties are in power.[3] Having tacitly accepted the People's Democratic Party of Afghanistan (PDPA) as a ruling communist party—however fragmented and internally riven it was in practice—Gorbachev, like his three predecessors, seemed at times to have accepted Afghanistan as part of this 'socialist world'. In the past, such status could have suggested the applicability of the 'Brezhnev Doctrine' of 'limited sovereignty', guaranteeing Soviet support, including direct military involvement by the Soviet Army or a surrogate, such as the Cubans or the Poles, to protect the 'achievements of socialism' and prevent the country from being detached from the Soviet sphere of influence and control by any external or internal threat. Under the Brezhnev Doctrine, such a country thus became, in effect, part of the Soviet 'patrimony', to be handed over to succeeding cohorts of Soviet leaders as part of their share of the world. And in a kind of geopolitical 'mercantilism' the inbuilt ideological and political motivation of Soviet foreign policy was constantly to try to increase this share. Yielding to internal or external pressure to give up any part of this patrimony was heretofore unthinkable, a sign of the unworthiness and incompetence of the leadership team which allowed it to happen. That was the clear message of the decisive Soviet actions in Eastern Europe in 1948, 1953, 1956, 1968 and (via General Jaruzelski) 1981. It also goes a long way toward explaining the decision to invade Afghanistan in December 1979 to protect the achievements of the 'April 1978 Revolution'. Reformist communist party leaders and Polish Solidarity spokesmen who argued for greater autonomy for their respective countries perhaps naively failed to understand this axiom of Soviet behaviour toward these 'special' kinds of allies. The abandonment of Afghanistan, if carried through to its manifest conclusion, is further evidence that a major change *may* be at hand in the code of Soviet foreign policy conduct.

Merely to state the question in these terms suggests the importance of Soviet theoretical distinctions among different kinds and levels of alliance. In broad terms, there are three classes of states with which the USSR has maintained alliances of one kind or another: (1) non-socialist states (2) states with a 'socialist orientation' and (3) communist party-ruled states. The first group of states, which today includes India, Syria, Iraq, Libya and South Yemen and once included Egypt and Somalia as well, involves the least degree of Soviet military commitment in the event of direct attack. Beyond the provision of military supplies and associated military-technical training and advice, the actual extent of Soviet commitment is deliberately kept vague to leave Soviet options open and keep potential enemies guessing. As in the Israeli-Egyptian 'war of attrition' of 1970 and the Indo-Pakistani war over Bangladesh in 1971, limited Soviet forces may be actively involved, but that is not usually the case. The distinguishing feature of these kinds of alliances is the implicitly weak ideological commitment of the Soviet Union toward the alliance partners. In developing its relations with them Moscow has had to overcome previous distaste for regimes which, although 'progressive' in declared socio-political orientation, have regularly treated their respective communist parties very roughly.[4] Having run the gamut of trying to justify support for the leaders of these regimes or movements by classifying them as, successively, 'national bourgeoisie', 'national democrats' and 'revolutionary democrats', the Soviets seem finally to have given up the quest for consistent ideological justification and now tacitly accept these persons for what they are: political opportunists who are willing, for one reason or another, to take the Soviet side in the East-West conflict. Such a limited intensity of mutual commitment obviously has its advantages at the present, more introspective stage of Soviet internal and external development. In fact, Moscow probably considers its links with

India as a model of the kind of relations it would like to see prevail with most countries outside of the 'socialist world' (and possibly even with some of the latter as well). India's support for the Soviet position at various stage of the Afghan venture, and especially for Moscow's scenario for extracting itself from the quagmire, has been worth its weight in gold—or MiG-29s or Charlie-Class nuclear attack submarines.

To see why the Indian relationship is relatively so propitious, it is necessary only to look at some of the problems the Soviet Union has been experiencing in its relations with the second class of allies, the states 'of socialist orientation'. These are states with which the Soviets have since the early 1950s had a kind of 'special relationship' based on ideological affinity and the sense of commitment that has heretofore applied. The leaders of these states or movements, heading what have come to be called 'Marxist-Leninist Vanguard Parties', characteristically proclaim themselves to be socialists and 'anti-imperialists' and pledge to follow a 'non-capitalist path of development'.[5] The latter obligation has entailed copying Soviet experience by the nationalisation of key sectors of the economy, collectivisation of agriculture, and the introduction of the main features of the Soviet system of political, economic, and social administration, such as central planning, a monopolistic one-party political order, and a 'revolutionary' class policy in the distribution of social opportunities and benefits. A sample of the countries falling within this classification presently would include Nicaragua in Latin America, Angola, Mozambique and Ethiopia in Africa, and The People's Democratic Republic of South Yemen, Laos, Kampuchea, and, of course, initially in 1978-79, Afghanistan in Asia.

The record of these countries has been a uniformly poor one. By the very radicalism of their internal 'socialist-orientation' programs they manage to alienate large parts of their domestic populations—and not only the proverbial 'class-alien elements'. In most cases they have succeeded in inciting the formation of hostile 'counterrevolutionary' movements, against whom the Soviets and their allies (mainly Cubans and East Germans) have ineluctably found themselves forced to take up arms in prolonged and seemingly unwinnable wars. These conflicts have often, furthermore, attracted the involvement of the West on the 'counterrevolutionary' side, encumbering Soviet efforts at negotiations on other, more central issues and parts of the world and raising the always latent threat of direct East-West military confrontation. Even where countries of this second category of alliances have 'successfully' made the transition to the third category of fully fledged socialist countries inhabiting the 'world of socialism', such as Cuba and the Socialist Republic of Vietnam, the Soviets can hardly consider the transition an unmixed blessing, for the residual revolutionary militancy and the ideological and/or geopolitical irredentism of such regimes continue to cause problems for Moscow in dealing with the West and with desirable Third-World negotiating partners such as the ASEAN countries. The Afghan experiment has seemed to epitomise virtually all of these difficulties for broader Soviet interests, particularly from the perspective of the 'new political thinking'.

The third class of Soviet allies are the communist party-ruled states proper. Among them, of course, are to be found countries that are only distantly linked, if at all, in a politico-military type of alliance relationship with the USSR. Yugoslavia, China, North Korea and Albania are communist party-ruled states which deny the existence of such a relationship and eschew the kind of mutual obligations with Moscow that apply in the case of the Warsaw Pact states, Cuba, Vietnam and the Mongolian People's Republic. Indeed, the type of mutual obligations entailed under the Brezhnev Doctrine—satellite fealty to enunciated principles and practices of Soviet-style socialism in return for Soviet political and economic assistance to the local party leaders whenever they run into trouble, as the model virtually guarantees that they will—apply only to the Warsaw Pact states and Mongolia, since only they are geographically and militarily susceptible to direct Soviet pressure. For a while they seemed to apply to Afghanistan as well.

At this point it is worthwhile emphasising the reciprocity of the obligations between the USSR and its alliance partners under the latter two classes of alliances. These allies abdicate a substantial part of their freedom of foreign and domestic action, but in turn they are the beneficiaries of a high degree of Soviet commitment to the survival of the particular regimes in question. Since many of the latter are periodically forced to fight for their very survival and since, under the circumstances, freedom of domestic and foreign action may seem a very abstract notion, it is not surprising that many of them evidently consider the trade-off to be highly advantageous. Indeed, given their political and ideological orientations, they probably tend to consider such a relationship rather more propitious than the nebulous alternative linkages offered by the main Western countries and their international groupings, such as the International Monetary Fund and the World Bank, which impose economic and political conditions that are even less desirable from their point of view.

The Decision to Withdraw and Its Implications

What the decision to withdraw Soviet troops from Afghanistan signifies in terms of the scheme presented in the preceding sections is a shift in the position of Afghanistan from third-category to second-category alliance status. More broadly still, it foreshadows the culmination of a process, dating back to the immediate post-Brezhnev period, of a reassessment of the validity of the special status of the second category of allies with a 'socialist orientation': that is, a tacit conflation of the first two categories, signifying a reduction in the level of Soviet economic, political and military obligation to states of the second category.[6]

There have been several indications of this shift in Soviet thinking. One of them is the elevation of the strategy of 'national reconciliation', which Gorbachev endorsed for Afghanistan during a visit by PDPA leader Dr Najibullah to Moscow in July 1987, to the status of a major normative principle of internal political and military conduct by Third-World states embroiled in civil or regional conflicts.[7] The important point is that this norm— the settlement of internal or regional disputes by peaceful political means and the integration of dissident, even avowedly anti-socialist, movements into the national political life—is meant to apply to second-category as well as first-category states.

It could plausibly be argued that this new policy is merely a reversion to the old Comintern strategy of the 'United Front'(both 'from above' and 'from below') and the 'Popular Front' of the 1920s and 1930s in a period of Soviet political weakness. There are also some important differences from the earlier situation, however. For one thing, in the present context the policy represents a shift from a position of perceived strength in terms of East-West military-political rivalry. Unlike the earlier situations, where a still weak Soviet Union was trying to create new positions of pro-Soviet support or defence against hostile forces, it means a retreat from already achieved positions, albeit not very stable ones. For another, the current policy is based on a much more pragmatic and sober consideration of the political, social and economic forces involved than was possible in the earlier periods.

In particular, the Soviets are now more inclined to consider the opportunity costs of maintaining their commitments to the states of 'socialist orientation', indeed, to the poorer parts of the Third World in general.[8] Arguments range from the utility for the Soviet Union, as a major exporter of fuels and raw materials, to be seen as a leader of the quest for a 'new international economic order'—which means abandoning identification with only a narrow range of Third-World countries—to targeting Soviet trade more heavily toward the rapidly developing 'newly industrialising states' such as South Korea, Singapore, Thailand and even Taiwan, which are capable of supplying the USSR with the kinds of medium- and high-tech products it requires for its own modernisation and consumerisation. In general, the aim is to reduce the ideologically inspired, benevolent-assistance complexion of Soviet dealings with the Third World in favour of a more mutually beneficial pattern of relationships—all part of the recognition under Gorbachev that the Soviet Union itself is in many respects closer to a Third-World than a developed socio-economic system.

Another important indication of the general shift in Soviet attitude toward the kind of open-ended commitment exemplified by Afghanistan (and probably Angola, Ethiopia and Kampuchea as well) was the publication of a series of articles suggesting that the Afghan adventure had been a mistake from the outset. Perhaps the most striking of these was the article in *Literaturnaia gazeta* on 17 February 1988 by the writer Aleksandr Prokhanov, a frequent observer of the situation in Afghanistan and renowned as a supporter of the Soviet involvement. In his article Prokhanov recalled how he had been won over to the communist credentials of the PDPA's seizure of power as early as April 1978 and was enthusiastic about the effort to protect its achievements during the upsurge of 'counterrevolutionary' activity in the following year. It was only later that he began to be disappointed at the successive PDPA leaders' loss of touch with Afghan realities and the party's increasing readiness to betray its own principles and compromise with its enemies![9]

In a way this was strange criticism, since the PDPA leaders, first, Babrak Karmal and then, Najibullah, had presumably been doing what their Soviet mentors had been telling them to do. Accordingly, the article could be regarded as orthodox ideological rationale for the pullout, addressed to conservative elements in the Soviet elite for whom the traditional arguments for supporting allies of 'socialist orientation' and led by 'Marxist-Leninist Vanguard Parties' still carried weight. Prokhanov's impeccable hard-line credentials support such an interpretation. On the other hand, his assertion that the PDPA had begun to go wrong shortly after the 'April Revolution' can be taken as broader criticism of 'Marxist-Leninist Vanguard Parties' and their lack of the discipline and programmatic rationality and consistency characteristic of genuine communist parties. Whatever the correct interpretation, the conclusion was clear: the Soviet invasion had been a mistake, and the Soviet Army had no further obligation or justification for shedding its blood in Afghanistan. A somewhat less problematical item was allowed to be published in the same journal a month later by Oleg Bogomolov, the Head of the Institute of Economics of the World Socialist System of the USSR Academy of Sciences. Bogomolov revealed that his Institute had warned of the 'futile and damaging nature' of Soviet military involvement in a submission to the top Kremlin leadership as early as January 20th, 1980, less than a month after the invasion.[10] Bogomolov disclosed that, besides Brezhnev himself, only the military seemed to be in favour of the incursion; the KGB specifically warned of the unwinnability of the war and of the likely costs to Soviet policy elsewhere.[11]

This scape-goating of Brezhnev and 'his' military advisers for the decision to invade was an easily recognisable Gorbachevian manoeuvre to set the stage for an abrupt shift in policy. He had done similar things to prepare for important changes in domestic policy. Once the decision to leave Afghanistan had been made, it seems to have been remarkably easy to carry it out: there was obviously plenty of public support for leaving and no great love lost for the hapless Afghan 'comrades' who were to be left in the lurch.[12] In a way, there seems to have been less agonising over the issue than was true of the US decision to abandon South

Vietnam. Note the following bland description of the decision-making process by Boris Piadyshev, Editor-in-Chief of the journal *International Affairs* and a member of the Collegium of the USSR Ministry of Foreign Affairs in April 1988, before the signing of the Geneva Accords: 'As regards the Soviet Union, we took a fresh look at the situation in Afghanistan and came to the conclusion that the conditions for pulling out were there. Our troops will leave Afghanistan. It would be better if this were done through the Geneva mechanism. It would be better if it came about with the United States and other countries showing understanding. But the knot will be undone in any event. Those who imagine that by making such a solution difficult they can bring about a situation in Afghanistan more favourable to them than now are wrong.'[13]

In short, the Soviet Union had decided to pull its troops out; the internal struggle with the *Mujahideen* would be up to the PDPA regime. Moscow had advised it to adopt a conciliatory policy toward its internal enemies, while retaining as much power as the central element of a future government as it could. Soviet diplomacy would strive to obtain as much recognition of the Najibullah Government's legitimacy by Pakistan and other interested parties as it could, hopefully with a modicum of US involvement as a guarantor of the status quo. Moscow would continue to furnish military and economic assistance as necessary. But as far as Gorbachev and his colleagues were concerned, direct Soviet participation in the war was essentially over. Recent events indicate that the same basic message, with suggestions of similar techniques for achieving a face-saving, second-best outcome, for example, the 'policy of national reconciliation', was apparently being recommended to other troubled or troublesome allies, namely, Angola, Vietnam (over Kampuchea) and Nicaragua.[14] It would be odd if similar processes were not in train in Ethiopia as well. The late Hafizullah Amin's confident assertion in Moscow at the 61st Anniversary celebration of the Great October Socialist Revolution in November 1978 that 'the Soviets will protect the [Afghan] Revolution'[15] had proven characteristically (for Amin) wrong. A new leadership team was in the saddle in Moscow.

Implications for Allies in the 'World of Socialism'

Our knowledge of the reaction by the Soviet Union's closest allies in the 'world of socialism' to the decision to withdraw from Afghanistan remains sketchy because of the paucity of serious assessments in the East European media. Although the matter was undoubtedly discussed in Warsaw Treaty Organisation forums, no joint declaration of Bloc states was issued, to my knowledge, and the type of coverage remained basically factual—mainly news agency reports transmitting the statements of Soviet and Afghan officials or laudatory comments by third parties. From the Soviet press one learned, for example, that the signing of the Geneva Accords on the 14th of April was enthusiastically received in Czechoslovakia, where its significance was compared with the Soviet-American INF Treaty. Both these treaties, according to the Czech youth newspaper *Mlada fronta* 'reflect the principles of the new political thinking and point to the fact that even the most complicated problems can be solved by way of negotiations.'[16] The Romanian party newspaper *Scinteia* was similarly cited as hailing the contribution of the Accords to the 'normalisation of the situation in the region', to an improvement in the climate of international relations, to 'strengthening confidence among countries and to the relaxation of international tensions'.[17] A Polish correspondent reported favourable Chinese reaction to Gorbachev's Tashkent meeting with Najibullah setting the schedule for withdrawal of Soviet troops. According to an official Xinhua statement, this would provide a good atmosphere for the Gorbachev-Reagan summit meeting in Moscow.[18] Most of the comments in the media of socialist countries were of this nature, usually quoting official sources or the opinions of officials directly involved in the negotiations rather than presenting original interpretative assessments.

Nevertheless, the infrequent editorials and signed articles that *did* appear suggested certain nuances of difference in the way the respective East European allies reacted to the Soviet pullout. It is possible to distinguish what could be broadly called liberal and conservative positions. The former essentially accepted the Gorbachevian rationale for the withdrawal but went further in the realism, not to say pessimism, of its assessment of the future

112

and in the assignment of blame for any future disaster primarily to the Afghans themselves, including the PDPA. The conservative position tended to replicate Soviet judgements of the situation, was perhaps less optimistic about the Afghan regime's prospects for survival without Soviet troops, but placed the major responsibility for an eventual collapse on Pakistan and the USA.

Of the three countries surveyed, Poland, Bulgaria and East Germany, the Poles provided by far the best coverage of the events leading up to and following the Geneva Accords. *Trybuna Ludu,* for example, carried an only slightly abridged version of Aleksandr Prokhanov's article in *Literaturnaia gazeta* featuring the argument that the Afghan adventure had been a grievous mistake, which would have 'painful after-effects' on the USSR, its culture, internal politics, social conditions and the life of a significant part of a whole generation of Soviet citizens.[19] In reporting the meeting between Gorbachev and Najibullah in Tashkent on 7 April, *Trybuna Ludu*, like other East European papers, noted the communiqué issued by the two leaders, point 5 of which stated that 'the problems of Afghanistan and their solutions are Afghanistan's own business and no one else's', to be solved by that country as an 'independent, non-aligned, neutral state'.[20] The implications of this formulation for autonomist forces in Eastern Europe were obvious, but no one seemed inclined to mention them.

The same paper published on 7 April a letter from Najibullah to UN Secretary General Pérez de Cuéllar stating that 'The Afghan Government is working to make the regularisation of the situation around Afghanistan a model for the solution of other regional conflicts.'[21] Following the signing of the Geneva Accords, a commentator for *Trybuna Ludu*, Zygmunt Slomkowski, after presenting a chronicle of events in Afghanistan since 1978, tried to justify the 'April Revolution' by describing the backwardness of the country 'even by Asian standards', but concluded that one could not rush the revolutionary process by pushing slogans and programs incomprehensible to the masses. He condemned the interference of the USA and other Western countries, as well as the intolerant Islamic fundamentalism of the *Mujahideen*, and praised the 'realism' of the PDPA and the USSR in acknowledging the complexity of the situation and agreeing to the withdrawal of

Soviet forces. And he ended with the pessimistic conclusion that the 'final chapter' of the April Revolution had still to be written. The outcome would depend on what the USA, Pakistan, Iran and the *Mujahideen* decided to do. The Afghan people, he said, had a 'great opportunity' to help themselves, but they must make use of it.[22]

Perhaps the most interesting and penetrating treatment of the events around the withdrawal appeared in the pages of the Polish weekly *Polityka*. Its correspondent, Jerzy Chocilowski, reported from Kabul in late April on the 'electrifying effect' of the news of the Soviet withdrawal, citing the 'many open questions' on the past, present and future of the country, despite the apparent initial optimism. There was no peace in Kabul, which was extremely dangerous after dark. Taxi drivers had to be avoided as potential spies of the *Mujahideen*. The Western-supplied Stinger and Blowpipe missiles had proven a big factor in changing the military balance, bringing the war to a 'bloody stalemate'. There was, he said, no sense in continuing it.

Chocilowski's frank assessment of the Geneva Accords was that they were historic, not so much for what they achieved, but as an expression of a 'new Soviet philosophy and practice of international relations'. His conclusion was particularly striking: 'It could be said—without thinking of the future—that it [the Geneva settlement] has more significance for East-West coexistence and thus for world security than it does for the Afghan drama'. For, he pointed out quite rightly, the agreement itself did not really bind anyone to do anything, neither the Afghans nor the Pakistanis. This placed a great responsibility on the two guarantors, the USA and the USSR. It would be a tragedy, he said, if the Afghan Revolution ended in a renewed outbreak of civil war. Whatever its faults and mistakes, the April Revolution accomplished something. Sooner or later, he concluded, the feudal and traditional order had to be overcome 'to bring Afghanistan into the modern world'.[23] A more pointed epitaph for a failed adventure would be difficult to imagine.

The Bulgarian and East German coverage was significantly less insightful and more manipulative. Reporting on a press conference by Najibullah a month before the Geneva signing, the Bulgarian Telegraph Agency, for example, stressed the Afghan leader's determination that his country solve its own problems.[24] Two days later a writer in *Rabotnichesko delo* repeated the increasingly popular formula of the Afghanistan solution as a model for the diplomatic solution of regional conflicts and 'small wars'.[25] Subsequent reports were characterised by a nagging conservative doubt that the stated Soviet objective of a peaceful, integral Afghanistan could be achieved because of the continued interference of Pakistan and the USA.[26] At the same time, the Bulgarians evidently did not wish to diverge too much from the Soviet position. A correspondent for *Rabotnichesko delo*, observing the first stage of the Soviet withdrawal in mid-May, denied that Afghanistan was being abandoned: 'On the contrary, now fraternal aid is entering a new stage, acquiring a new form'; and he noted increasing contacts between Soviet republics and individual Afghan provinces. Still, he warned, only time would tell whether peace was possible.[27] One interesting bit of information intended to show that the Afghan Army was capable of defeating the *Mujahideen* without Soviet assistance was the report that the PDPA had grown from 155000 to 205000 members in the period since 1 January 1987. Of this number fully 150000 were reported to be in the army and other military and security formations.[28]

The East Germans reflected what we have called the conservative position on the Soviet withdrawal, but their press coverage was generally non-committal, being limited to news agency reports with but one editorial exception. The latter was written on the occasion of the beginning of the Soviet troop withdrawal, which was said to 'show how earnest the Soviet Union is, with the consistent implementation of the Geneva Accords on Afghanistan, to contribute to the improvement of the situation in the world as a whole.' But it went on to point out that the Accords were not a 'one-way street'; all foreign interference had to cease.[29] East German News Agency (ADN) reports regularly condemned the US (and sometimes Pakistan as well) for continuing to interfere in Afghan affairs by sending in military equipment to the *Mujahideen*. In the latter part of July, for example, an ADN dispatch from Kabul reported the Afghan Government's rejection of the declared grounds for US aid to the 'rebels', and its contention that 'there can be nothing in common between support for terrorists and aid for an independent, sovereign and non-aligned state ...'[30] The report then went on to describe rocket attacks on residential areas of Kabul. While praising Soviet and Afghan intentions, the East Germans were

115

evidently none too confident of the ultimate success of the declared aims of the Soviet move. Unlike the Bulgarians, who saw some hope in the reports of dissension in the ranks of the *Mujahideen* and regarded this as a positive factor in the PDPA Government's ability to maintain power,[31] the East Germans apparently have few illusions on that score and, thus, may be considered 'purer' representatives of the conservative position.

What these admittedly random samplings of the East European press suggest is a spectrum of attitudes on the merits of the Soviet decision to withdraw. The Poles most clearly accepted the decision for what it was: a repudiation of a policy that was flawed from the outset and the sacrifice of the Afghan 'comrades' on the altar of broader Soviet interests. They had no implicit or explicit criticism of the decision. The Bulgarians and East Germans presumably disagreed with the decision and the assessment that the initial invasion was mistaken or that the war was unwinnable. The Bulgarians tried to put a positive face on the withdrawal by repeating without comment the Soviet assurances that Afghanistan was not being abandoned and that there was some hope of PDPA survival if only outside interference could be curbed. The East Germans did not even try to go that far. The decision was accepted, because it had to be, but there was no sense in trying to make a defeat look like anything else. The USA was the main culprit, but the USSR was also implicitly being criticised for proceeding with the withdrawal in the face of alleged Western violations of the Accords.

The principal implication of the Soviet decision for the East European allies was that the rules of the Soviet foreign policy game had been changed—for some of the players on the Soviet side, but not for others. The Soviet Union would no longer allow itself to be diverted from pursuing its objectives in the 'first two worlds' by endless, unwinnable, or even uneasily winnable, commitments in the 'third'. But it was clear that different rules applied to the Soviet allies in the second world, namely, the members of the Warsaw Treaty Organisation. There was ample evidence of Soviet determination to reinforce, if anything, the linkages with these countries.[32]

Facile extensions of the 'lessons of Afghanistan' to Eastern Europe, and especially the issue of the maintenance of large bodies of Soviet troops in all of the countries except Romania and Bulgaria, seem to ignore one fact of which Gorbachev is

116

well aware: the current crop of East European communist leaders *rely* on Soviet support. Most of them realise that without the presence or threat of Soviet troops in their countries, they would have a difficult time maintaining themselves in power. Even non-Warsaw Treaty Organisation member Yugoslavia and, conceivably Ceausescu in Romania, depend on the bogeyman of Soviet intervention to ward off liberalising challenges to the existing Marxist-Leninist order. No one among the present leaders, or anyone likely to appear on the scene in the near future, can be expected to press for the kind of status being granted to Afghanistan as an 'independent, non-aligned, neutral state'. Even if someone among them were tempted to 'chance his arm' on such a change in status, the obligations under the Warsaw Pact, COMECON and various bilateral linkages with the USSR clearly militate against it.

Conclusions

Gorbachev's decision to withdraw Soviet troops from Afghanistan marked an important turning point in the evolution of Soviet foreign policy. Particularly in regard to policy in the Third World it marked a decisive shift away from the policy of the Brezhnev years to seek out targets of opportunity to increase the compass of Soviet power by the use of the USSR's expanding military power, regardless of the economic and diplomatic costs. The shift marked the abandonment for the foreseeable future of the strategy of seeking allies among what we have called 'second-category' partners—countries of 'socialist orientation', headed by Marxist-Leninist Vanguard Parties—in favour of less ideologically committed, but economically and politically more profitable connections with more stable and politically viable allies in the Third World in general. The assistance afforded by India under Rajiv Gandhi in easing the Soviet Union out of Afghanistan is a case in point.[33]

Being bogged down in countries like Afghanistan, Angola and Ethiopia, and somewhat less directly, in Kampuchea and Nicaragua, not only encumbered Soviet relations with China and the West, but also placed it in an unwontedly defensive position in the United Nations and major parts of the Third World itself. The strategy of disengagement through the establishment of governments of 'national reconciliation' in its erstwhile second-category allies is emerging as a general model for managing local conflicts in the Third World susceptible to superpower confrontation in order to clear the atmosphere for Gorbachev's brand of flexible main-stream diplomacy under the 'new political thinking'.

The role clearly envisaged for the East European allies in the new thinking is as part of the Soviet economic and political team, not as part of the baggage of 'stagnation' that is being repudiated. That is why Gorbachev is pressuring them, over considerable reluctance in some countries, to emulate the Soviet Union in implementing the programs of *perestroika* and *glasnost'*: to compel them to contribute more fully to the broader objective of making the 'world of socialism' a more effective and attractive force in the continuing contest with the world of capitalism for global influence. The lesson of Afghanistan is something Gorbachev is forcing all of them to learn. As we have seen, some have accepted the consequent downgrading of the hallowed imperatives of 'proletarian internationalism' more gracefully than others.

Afghanistan has turned out to be Moscow's 'Vietnam' after all. It would probably be unwise for the West to emulate the Soviet Union of the mid-1970s and draw the wrong conclusions from the adversary's obvious present discomfiture.

FOOTNOTES

[1] These expectations and assumptions are set forth at length in Gorbachev's book *Perestroika: New Thinking for our Country and the World* (London: Collins, 1987), especially Part II, 'New Thinking and the World'.

[2] *Ibid.*, p.165.

[3] In the past such countries have been officially referred to variously as the 'socialist camp', the 'socialist commonwealth' (*sotsialisticheskoe sodruzhestvo*) and the 'world socialist system'. The rather less precise formula of the 'socialist world' is more in keeping with the greater flexibility and ideologically less constraining policy posture connoted by Gorbachev's 'new political thinking'.

[4] For a classic analysis of the early problems of Soviet relations with non-communist third-world countries and movements see John H. Kautsky's *Moscow and the Communist Party of India: A Study in the Postwar Evolution of International Communist Strategy* (New York: John Wiley &

Sons, 1956). For a more recent treatment of these relationships see Edward Taborsky, *Communist Penetration of the Third World*. (New York: Robert Speller & Sons, 1973), especially Chapters 4-6. A collection illustrating the evolution of Western perspectives on these issues, this time with a comparative regional focus, is Robert H. Donaldson (ed.), *The Soviet Union in the Third World* (Boulder: Westview Press, 1981), which even has a chapter (no. 11) on the Soviet invasion of Afghanistan, much of which makes quaint reading today. More recent still are the books by Jerry F. Hough, *The Struggle for the Third World: Soviet Debates and American Options* (Washington, D.C.: The Brookings Institition, 1986); and by Andrzej Korbonski and Francis Fukuyama (eds.), *The Soviet Union and the Third World: The Last Three Decades* (Ithaca and London: Cornell University Press, 1987).

5   For a good discussion of the evolution and use of this concept see Francis Fukuyama, 'Soviet Strategy in the Third World', in Korbonski and Fukuyama (eds.), *op. cit.*, pp.30-42.

6   Fukuyama, *op. cit.*, pp.42-45, makes the same point, referring to Gorbachev's playing down of the differences among various kinds of Third-World countries in his Report to the 27th Congress of the CPSU. Fukuyama did not think Gorbachev would be able to cast off the ideological motivations of the special relationship with the states of 'socialist orientation', but that was before the decision to withdraw from Afghanistan.

7   Gennadi Musalyan and Aleksandr Sukhopanov, 'Afghanistan: Following the Road of Goodwill', *International Affairs* (Moscow), no.1, January 1988, p.123. See, also, for example, the interview with Soviet Deputy Minister of Foreign Affairs V.F. Petrovskii in the journal *MEMO*, no.4, April 1988, pp.3-9, especially p.5, where Petrovskii is quoted as saying: 'At the session [of the UN] attitudes were dominant in favour of the un-blocking of conflict and crisis situations, and the policy of national reconciliation, initiated in the Republic of Afghanistan, was accepted as a basic model for the regularisation of conflict and crisis situations'.

8   For conflicting views of these problems, with, however, similar conclusions regarding Soviet policy—that is, to get more out of trade with the Third World, particularly the so-called 'newly industrialised states', see N. Shmelev, '"Tretii mir" i mezhdunarodnye ekonomicheskie otnosheniia', *MEMO*, no.9, September 1987, pp.12-24; R. Avakov, 'Novoe myshlenie i problemy izucheniia razvivaiushchikhsia stran', *MEMO*, no.11, November 1987, pp.48-62; and L. Zevin, 'Nekotorye voprosy ekonomicheskogo sotrudnichestva SSSR s razvivaiushchimisia stranami', *MEMO*, no.3, March 1988, pp.41-51.

9   Aleksandr Prokhanov, 'Afganskie voprosy', *Literaturnaia gazeta*, 17 February 1988, pp.1, 9.

10 Oleg Bogomolov, 'Kto zhe oshibalsia?', *Literaturnaia gazeta*, 16 March 1988, p.10.

11 *Ibid*. On the KGB's position, see the testimony of the defector Vladimir Kuzichkin, 'Coups and Killings in Kabul', *Time*, 22 November 1982, pp.35-36.

12 For a report on Soviet public opinion on the war see Sallie Wise, "'A War Should Never Have Happened": Soviet Citizens Assess the War in Afghanistan', *Radio Liberty Research*, RL 226/88, 1 June 1988.

13 'International Affairs Guest Club', *International Affairs*, no.4, April 1988, p.9. The occasion was a roundtable discussion with a group of Western newsmen in the editorial offices of the journal.

14 The USSR is reported by US officials to have applied 'pressure on Cuba and Angola' to reach agreement, because of Soviet financial problems and a desire to 'reduce their involvement in Third World conflicts', 'S Africa, Angola and Cuba announce end to "hostilities"', *The Sydney Morning Herald*, 10 August 1988, p.11.

15 Quoted by Shirin Tahir-Kheli, in 'The Soviet Union in Afghanistan: Benefits and Costs', in Donaldson, (ed.), *op. cit.*, p.230.

16 'Uspekh dal'novidnoi politiki', *Pravda*, 20 April 1988, p.4.

17 *Ibid*.

18 Krystyna Szelestowska, 'Reakcje chinskie', *Trybuna Ludu*, 12 April 1988, p.6.

19 'Afganskie problemy', *Trybuna Ludu*, 27-28 February 1988, p.7.

20 'Spotkanie Gorbaczow-Nadzibullah', *Trybuna Ludu*, 8 April 1988, pp.1, 6.

21 'List Nadzibullah do Perez de Cuellara', *Trybuna Ludu*, 7 April 1988, p.6.

22 Zygmunt Słomkowski, 'Afganistan 1978-1988', *Trybuna Ludu*, 27 April 1988, p.5.

23 Jerzy Chocilowski, 'Nadzieja i niepewnosc', *Polityka*, 23 April 1988, pp.1, 12.

24 'Republika Afganistan otstoiava printsipna realistichna pozitsiia', *Rabotnichesko delo*, 15 March 1988, p.5.

25 Volodia Stratiev, 'Preduprezhdenieto', *Rabotnichesko delo*, 17 March 1988, p.5.

26 See, for example, Volodia Stratiev, 'Formulata na napred"ka', *Rabotnichesko delo*, 9 April 1988, p.5; Atanas Atanasov, 'Edinstveniat brod', *Rabotnichesko delo*, 20 May 1988, p.5.

27 Valeri Naidenov, 'Zapochni izteglianeto na s"vetskite voiski', *Rabotnichesko delo*, 16 May 1988, pp.1, 6.

28 Atanas Atanasov, 'Aktiven dialog i razumni kompromisi', *Rabotnichesko delo*, 16 May 1988, p.6; also, Volodia Stratiev, 'Protses"t na natsionalno pomirenie s"zdava usloviia za mirno razvitie', *Rabotnichesko delo*, 10 July 1988, p.4.

29 'Kernpunkt: Schluss mit der Einmischung in Afghanistan', *Neues Deutschland*, 17 May 1988, p.2.

30 'Afghanistan fordert USA zur Einhaltung der Vertraege auf', *Neues Deutschland*, 20 July 1988, p.5.

31 See, for example, Volodia Stratiev, 'Protses"t na natsionalno pomirenie s"zdava usloviia za mirno razvitie', *Rabotnichesko delo*, 10 July 1988, p.4.

32 See, for example, Robert F. Miller, 'The Soviet Union and Eastern Europe: Genuine Integration at Last?', in R.F. Miller, J.H. Miller and T.H. Rigby

(eds.), *Gorbachev at the Helm: A New Era in Soviet Politics?* (London and Sydney: Croom Helm, 1987) pp.214-234, where various new techniques for intensifying integrationist tendencies within COMECON are discussed.

33 Gandhi's pledge during Najibullah's visit to India in May 1988 to support his efforts to maintain himself in power with economic aid, technical assistance, and diplomatic support—for example, by agreeing to act as an intermediary with ex-king Zahir Shah and other exiled Afghan politicians and by applying pressure on Pakistan—is reported approvingly in a Bulgarian Telegraph Agency report in *Rabotnichesko delo*, 7 May 1988, p.4 and in an article by Iordan Bozhilov, 'Nova stranitsa v otnosheniiata', *Rabotnichesko delo*, 8 May 1988, p.5.

8

Afghanistan and Sino-Soviet Relations

Leslie Holmes

Of one aspect of Sino-Soviet relations we can be certain: the Soviet withdrawal of troops from Afghanistan will not *of itself* be sufficient to allay long-standing Chinese fears about Soviet global—especially Asian—hegemonic intentions. Nor will it alter the fact that the People's Republic of China (PRC) is fully aware that it must be careful to balance improvements in relations with the USSR against its strategic and economic interest in maintaining or even improving its relationship with the capitalist West, especially the USA.

In any assessment of likely future developments in the Sino-Soviet relationship, it is important to consider at least the two issues other than Afghanistan that the Chinese have long and explicitly maintained must be resolved before any fundamental improvement in Sino-Soviet relations can occur—namely Soviet support of the Vietnamese occupation of Kampuchea and the large Soviet military presence just over China's borders. The Chinese have made it clear that the Afghanistan issue is less important to them certainly than the first of these and, possibly, than the second—although, as shall be demonstrated, the Afghan question cannot be completely separated from the Soviet military encirclement issue. The last point notwithstanding, Klintworth is thus in my view correct when he argues that 'China in fact no longer regards Afghanistan with the same degree of apprehension about Soviet encirclement as it did in 1979'[1].

But to consider *only* the 'three obstacles' is insufficient for a full analysis of the current state of Sino-Soviet relations. The relationship is a complex one, and cannot be understood without some reference to both Moscow's and Beijing's relationships to other third countries (for example the USA), plus cultural, ideological, strategic, territorial, economic and other factors. Before addressing the question of Afghanistan, I shall first remind the reader of the background to the current situation and then analyse recent developments.

The Sino-Soviet Relationship to 1985[2]

The Sino-Soviet conflict began to emerge in the 1950s, became very overt in the 1960s, and festered throughout the 1970s. In the 1980s, there were signs that the two giants of the communist world had grown more willing than they had been for many years to work at overcoming their differences; this became particularly evident after Gorbachev's accession to power in 1985. Even so, as recently as 1984 an article in *Beijing Review* claimed that, despite recent negotiations, 'the nature of the Sino-Soviet relationship remains unchanged', and Chinese leader Deng Xiaoping in 1988 made it clear that the USSR still needed to meet certain conditions before a summit between him and Gorbachev could take place.[3] Before an analysis of the developments since Gorbachev took office, a very brief history of the Sino-Soviet dispute is appropriate.

When Mao Zedong came to power in 1949, he did so almost in spite of Stalin. Stalin had maintained an ambivalent attitude towards the Chinese communists since the 1920s, and was urging caution on Mao in his dealings with the Guomindang well into 1949; the Chinese communists owed very little to the Soviets for their successful takeover. Mao never forgot this, as revealed in the fact that in 1962 he traced the Sino-Soviet dispute back to 1945, when Stalin had urged him to collaborate with Chiang Kai-shek.[4] Nevertheless, Mao respected many of Stalin's ideas and policies, especially the concept of 'socialism in one country'. He also admired many of the Soviet achievements. Largely for these reasons, early communist China was highly emulative of the Soviet Union, and signed a Friendship Treaty with Moscow in 1950. But following Stalin's death in 1953, the situation slowly began to change. The Chinese were already disappointed at what they considered to be insufficient support from the Soviets in the fight against the West during the Korean War (1950-1953); over the next few years, a number of other issues were to be added to this list. But the growing dissatisfaction was not unilateral. For instance, the Soviets were irritated by the Chinese in 1955, when Beijing made it clear that it did not feel the Soviets should attend the Bandung Conference, since this was supposed to be for African and Asian states only. In fact, the qualifications for attendance were less to do with geography than with economic levels of development, and China argued that it had far more in common with the Third World countries of Africa and Asia than did the highly industrialised USSR. But the Soviets perceived that there was more to the Chinese position than Beijing was revealing. Moscow seems to have believed that the Chinese were trying to increase their influence in the Third World, and the Soviets retaliated by trying to improve relations with other Asian states—including Afghanistan. Apparently they believed that the Chinese would, if given the opportunity, attempt to construct satellites similar to the USSR's own in Eastern Europe. The Soviets had not demonstrated any major interest in Asia thitherto, but, as they believed they saw China attempting to increase its influence in the region—sometimes by force, as with India in 1954—so they increased their activities.

Although the Chinese communist leadership initially supported Khrushchev's de-Stalinisation (which became overt in February 1956), Mao had by late-1957 changed his position and called for an ending of Soviet attacks on Stalin. The Chinese now started to accuse the Soviets of revisionism—to which the USSR responded by condemning Chinese dogmatism, leading to major differences between the two sides.[5] The mounting tensions burst into public view in April 1960, when the Chinese published a series of highly critical articles in which they accused the Soviets of having renounced their original Leninist aims.[6] The Soviets responded by withdrawing economic aid and advisers to China later in the year, leaving many major projects in which the

Soviets had been involved incomplete. The dispute was now visible to all. One of the most serious ramifications of the dispute emerged in 1962, when the Soviets supported a non-communist power (India) in its war with a communist power (the PRC).

Although the change of Soviet leadership in 1964 led to hopes in some quarters of an improvement in Sino-Soviet relations, this did not materialise. Mao was in a radical frame of mind—as reflected in the 'Great Proletarian Cultural Revolution'—and in no mood to start compromising with the Soviets. In fact, relations worsened still further in the late 1960s, culminating in border fighting between Chinese and Soviet troops on the Ussuri river in 1969. This appeared at the time to be so serious that some commentators felt it could develop into a full-scale Sino-Soviet war.[7] Partially because both sides realised how easily the situation might escalate, the border fighting was in fact short-lived.

The Chinese now slowly began to reassess their attitudes towards the West, which had practical ramifications for the Sino-Soviet dispute. Hitherto, Chinese policy towards the capitalist world had been unrelentingly hostile; largely under the influence of Premier Zhou Enlai, they began to warm to the West, especially to the USA. To some extent, this change reflected Chinese fears of the possible effects on China of the growing rapprochement between Moscow and Washington,[8] although it had also to be seen in the light of improving relations between the USSR and Western Europe following Brandt's accession to power in 1969 and his emphasis on *Ostpolitik*. The changes also reflected the growing Chinese fears of the conventional and nuclear weapons build-up in the USSR. The new Chinese policy was welcomed by the West; the US was anxious to use the Sino-US rapprochement as a lever in its negotiations with the USSR.[9] Signs of the fundamental change in attitude in both East and West included the admission of China to the UN in 1971 and President Nixon's visit to China in 1972. Thus the bilateral Sino-Soviet relationship had now changed into a trilateral one involving the West, with each communist state attempting to gain support from a (capitalist) third party.

Mao's death in September 1976 soon led to speculation that the Sino-Soviet relationship could change significantly. In fact, the Chinese initially seemed to be so preoccupied with their domestic political arrangements that the relationship with

Moscow (and as a corollary with Washington) was not a major focus of attention. But, as Deng consolidated power, signs began to emerge of a possible improvement in relations; many Western observers felt that Deng's more pragmatic approach to politics in general would probably result in a less hostile approach towards Moscow. Despite some very real set-backs and continuing tensions, this is in fact what has happened.

The beginning of the new phase has been traced back to 1979.[10] At that time, the Soviets urged the Chinese to renew the 1950 Sino-Soviet Treaty of Friendship; China refused, but agreed to reconsider its relationship with the Soviets provided the latter were prepared to discuss a range of Chinese concerns in addition to the question of the Sino-Soviet border. The situation appeared set to improve. But the Soviet intervention in Afghanistan led to a rapid deterioration in relations between Beijing and Moscow once again. In hindsight, however, this appears to have been a large hiccough; Afghanistan never has been the major issue from the Chinese perspective.

The Chinese began a major reassessment of foreign policy in 1981, one major ramification of which was that Beijing now started to view the two superpowers more equally. The USA was perceived more critically than before (largely because of the Taiwan issue and the strongly anti-communist rhetoric of President Reagan), whereas the USSR was seen in a less negative light. Expressed crudely, China was pursuing a policy of 'equidistance'—that is, the position that the superpowers were virtually as bad as each other, but that it had to maintain a working relationship with both. Moscow was quick to recognise this change. In a major speech in Tashkent in March 1982, Brezhnev declared that the USSR was prepared to discuss the border issue with China—at the same time as he stressed that the USSR, unlike the USA, did not pursue a 'Two-Chinas' policy.[11] But the Chinese were still wary. In his speech to the 12th Chinese Communist Party (CPC) Congress in September 1982, Hu Yaobang made it quite clear that there were fundamental differences between the Chinese and the Soviet perspectives on foreign policy: 'We do not station a single soldier abroad, nor have we occupied a single inch of foreign land. We have never infringed upon the sovereignty of another country, or imposed an unequal relationship upon it.'[12] He went on to state explicitly that Sino-Soviet relations were as they were because of the USSR's 'hegemonist policy' and that 'deeds, rather than words, are important'.[13]

This said, the Chinese *were* willing to start negotiations with the Soviets concerning a normalisation of their relationship. The first round of such twice-yearly talks took place in October 1982, and have continued ever since (the 12th round took place in June 1988). This is of relevance to the Afghanistan issue, since the Chinese had at one point made it a precondition of such talks that the Soviets remove all troops from Afghanistan.

Developments since 1985

At the 27th Congress of the Communist Party of the Soviet Union in February 1986, Gorbachev described the potential for cooperation with Chinese as 'enormous', but also referred to differences between the two countries, in particular on international affairs.[14] Like his predecessors, Gorbachev emphasised that cooperation between the two communist giants had to be 'without prejudice to third countries'—a clear indication that the Soviet leader was still not prepared to make major concessions on the issues that were blocking a *fundamental* improvement in Sino-Soviet relations—including Afghanistan. At about the same time, in his statement of 15 January 1986 on nuclear weapons, Gorbachev described the USSR as 'a major Asian power'—hardly the sort of rhetoric that could be expected to allay Chinese fears. The world had to wait another three months for signs of a real change on the part of the Soviets.

By July 1986, Gorbachev had decided that the time was ripe for a major reassessment of Soviet foreign policy. In the all-important Vladivostok speech of 28 July 1986, the first major signs in years of a fundamental shift in Soviet policy in Asia became visible. This landmark speech is a long and complex document, and all that can be done here is to isolate those elements of it that bear directly on our particular concern. In order to assess the importance of the document, this is an appropriate juncture at which to analyse what the Chinese have throughout the 1980s been claiming are the three main obstacles to a really significant improvement in Sino-Soviet relations— namely the Soviet military presence along the Chinese border,

Soviet occupation of Afghanistan, and Soviet support for the Vietnamese occupation of Kampuchea.

The Sino-Soviet border, at well over 6000 kilometres, is the world's longest land-based frontier between two states. Although the Soviets have withdrawn many of their troops from the Ussuri and Amur regions since the 1969 clashes, there has been a general build-up of Soviet troops and weaponry (both conventional and nuclear) in the Soviet Far East in recent years, which has not been conducive to an improvement in Sino-Soviet relations. The Chinese have made it clear that the presence of an estimated 65000 troops in the People's Republic of Mongolia—allegedly a sovereign state, and not apparently under any imminent threat either from external or domestic forces—is particularly intolerable.

The second issue, and our primary concern, is Afghanistan. As argued earlier, Afghanistan has in the author's view been the least important of the three obstacles from Beijing's perspective—at least in recent years. To a very limited extent, its inclusion in the Chinese list of obstacles is because the Soviets themselves put it on the agenda, in that the USSR argued at the time of its invasion of Afghanistan that one of the reasons for the intervention was the threat Beijing posed to Kabul. The Chinese have not historically devoted much attention to Afghanistan[15]; their main interest in the region in recent decades has been Pakistan, and concerns with Afghanistan must be seen for much of the post Second World War era principally in the context of relations with Islamabad.

But to argue that Afghanistan is now the least important issue is quite different from saying that it is of no or only marginal significance. There is at least one aspect of the Afghan issue which proved of some importance to the PRC, at least in the view of several Western commentators. Since it relates to the first obstacle (that is, Soviet military presence on China's borders), this issue—Soviet presence in the Wakhan Corridor— needs to be examined in some detail. If one examines a map of Afghanistan and its neighbours, one notices in the northeast corner of the country a long, thin strip that looks like an appendage—perhaps a 'sore thumb' would be more appropriate—to the main body of the country. This strip—the approximately 300 kilometre-long Wakhan Corridor—never exceeds 65 kilometres across, and in many parts is less than 20 kilometres wide. It is bounded to the north by the USSR, to the south by Pakistan, and to the east by the PRC. Indeed, the 60 kilometre strip that borders China is the sum total of the Sino-Afghan frontier.

Until 1980, the Wakhan Corridor had been under Afghan rule since the 1895 Afghan-Russian border settlement between the British and the Russians; the settlement, which was accepted reluctantly by the Afghans and almost ignored by the Chinese, followed disputes over the area that had been manifest since 1873.[16] But Soviet troops began to occupy the corridor in May 1980; at some unspecified date late in 1980, the Soviets probably took full administrative control of the area, although they never publicly acknowledged the fact.[17] From that time, the eastern half was out-of-bounds for almost all Afghans, and there were unconfirmed reports that the Soviets established two military camps, one signals intelligence site and an undetermined number of missile sites there.[18] One interesting fact in this connection is that Moscow and Kabul signed a border treaty formalising 'the existing guarded boundary', and specifically relating to the Wakhan Corridor, on 16 June 1981; given that there had been an undisputed agreement for this area since 1895, Amstutz is justified in questioning why another agreement was deemed necessary unless there were a change of boundaries—almost certainly to the Soviets' advantage—or, at the least, of sovereignty in the area.[19]

The Chinese did not appear to react very strongly, if at all[20], to the reports of Soviet annexation of the Corridor; from one perspective, their border with Afghanistan had been formally agreed upon in November 1963, and the Soviets were in no position to alter this without Chinese involvement. In short, the Chinese either simply did not acknowledge the change, or else were not particularly concerned by it. In a sense, the claims that sovereignty in the area had changed were far more embarrassing to the Kabul regime than threatening to the Chinese, and in December 1982, Babrak Karmal explicitly and publicly denied that the USSR had incorporated any Afghan territory.[21] Another factor to bear in mind is that it is from some perspectives preferable for the Chinese to have Soviets across the border from Xinjiang than *Mujahideen*; after all, there is a sizeable number of Muslims in Xinjiang, and they might be at least inspired by the success of Afghan *Mujahideen* if not actually in contact with them. The Chinese ambivalence on this is captured well by Segal, who writes: 'China is impressed by the triumph of nationalism in a small neighbour of the Soviet Union [that is, Afghanistan - LH] over the might of the Red Army. But it is also concerned that the power of such nationalism, when coupled with a potent religion, can defeat the appeal of modernising communism'.[22]

Does all this mean that the Wakhan Corridor is, despite the view of some western observers, essentially of no interest to the Chinese? This would be going too far. Until the Soviets occupied the corridor, it is widely believed that the Chinese used it as their main conduit for supplying arms and materials to the Afghan resistance movement. Although the Chinese do not appear to have been the major supplier of arms to the resistance—the *Mujahideen* claim that most of their weapons are obtained from raids on Soviet stores, Soviet defectors, and Soviet captives, whilst Egypt, the USA and Pakistan have all probably supplied more than the Chinese—they had seen it as in their interest to support the resistance fighters.[23] The closing off of the Wakhan Corridor was not a major problem for the Chinese, however, who seemed to have re-routed their supplies through Peshawar in Pakistan. A potentially more significant problem was that, according to Western intelligence reports, the Soviets from 1980 built all-weather roads in the corridor that would permit rapid deployment of Soviet troops to either the Pakistani or Chinese borders.[24] However, it seems that the Chinese were not overly concerned by this factor either, and made more of the threat this posed to Pakistan than to themselves.[25] A third factor requires us to ask why the Soviets wanted to occupy the Wakhan Corridor in the first place. One reason may well have been to cut off Chinese arms supplies; this factor has been considered above. Related to this is the fact that the area was at one time a stronghold of two radical Afghan groups, the *Shu'la-i-Jawed* (Eternal Flame) and the *Setem-i-Melli* (Against Oppression of the Nation).[26] Both of these, dating from the late-1960s, were more or less Maoist, and very anti-superpower.[27]

Many former members of *Shu'la-i-Jawed* and *Setem-i-Melli* formed a new group—*SAMA* (acronym for the Afghan People's Liberation Organisation)—in the Spring of 1979.[28] This became a dominant force in the United National Front (established January 1980) which for a while played a significant role in the anti-

Soviet struggle. The fact that many members of *SAMA* were once Maoist was not what worried the Soviets; after all, the Chinese themselves had largely rejected Maoism by 1980, and *SAMA* had expressed its desire to avoid contact with China.[29] Rather, the problem was that many of these resistance fighters were Tajik Muslims, who the Soviets almost certainly feared would try to incite unrest amongst Soviet Tajiks—Tajikistan is the Soviet republic bordering the Wakhan Corridor. The Soviets *may* also have wanted to maximise their opportunities for monitoring the 1979 Sino-American listening post in Xinjiang (the autonomous region immediately adjacent to the Wakhan Corridor). Whilst this is possible, another glance at the map will reveal that the Soviets could just as easily monitor from Tajikistan; given the rugged and inhospitable terrain of the Wakhan Corridor, it is not the case that locating a monitoring station there would clearly be easier than in the Tajik mountainous regions. The Chinese have a nuclear test site at Lop Nor in Xinjiang—but this is a long way from the Wakhan Corridor. It thus seems that we are back with the dated argument that the Soviets occupied to cut off arms supply routes and perhaps to give them better long-term access to Pakistan.

The third obstacle is in many ways currently the most important of the three from Beijing's perspective. When the Vietnamese began their invasion of Kampuchea—on Christmas Day 1978—they were seeking not only to replace a genocidal maniac with someone better disposed towards themselves, but also to depose a regime that was both anti-Vietnamese and *basically* pro-Chinese.[30] Anyone who has visited history museums in Vietnam in recent years will be aware of the deep-seated, centuries-old hostility of the Vietnamese towards the Chinese. This feeling is mutual, and one cannot begin to understand the tensions between Vietnam and China without this historical-cultural perspective. Vietnam has claimed it fears Chinese designs in Indochina; China retorts that it has no recent history of expansion, and that the Vietnamese, working with the Soviets, are seeking to expand their influence in the region so that China is surrounded by pro-Soviet (and hence, at least until recently, potentially anti-Chinese) regimes. In a sense it is the *matrioshka* syndrome; Vietnam feels threatened by a much larger neighbour, but that larger neighbour itself feels threatened by an even larger imperial neighbour.

How did Gorbachev's Vladivostok speech relate to the 'three obstacles'? In terms of military build-ups and Mongolia, Gorbachev stated explicitly that the USSR, in consultation with the Mongolian leadership, was now examining the possibilities of withdrawal of 'a considerable number' of Soviet troops from the People's Republic of Mongolia.[31] Moreover, Gorbachev stated that the USSR was ready to discuss with China a more general reduction in the number of troops stationed on the Sino-Soviet border.[32] Gorbachev actually concluded his analysis of concrete measures to be adopted in Asia by considering Afghanistan. He stated that there would soon be a start on the withdrawal of Soviet troops; six regiments were to returned to the USSR by the end of 1986.[33] Although the Soviets had previously referred to the possibilities of bringing back their troops (for example at the 27th CPSU Congress[34]), this had neither come from the General Secretary before nor been as specific. In this sense, this was—at least symbolically—a major step forward. Indeed, in arguing in his discussion of Afghanistan that 'actions should lie behind words', it was as if Gorbachev were directly responding to Hu's comments at the 12th CPC Congress. As for the third issue—the Soviet leader made it clear that any resolution of this would depend on a normalisation of Sino-Vietnamese relations, and that such an improvement was an issue for Beijing and Hanoi to settle between themselves.[35] He also made a veiled reference to the Sino-Vietnamese border skirmishes since 1979 when he referred to the need for a 'border of peace and good neighbourliness' once again between the PRC and the SRV. In short, he was placing much of the onus for the solution to this problem back on the Chinese. Although Gorbachev did not express it in these terms, he was highlighting a contradiction in Chinese policy—one that has in my view not been picked up sufficiently by Western observers. This is that the Chinese simultaneously condemn Soviet hegemonism and interference in others' affairs, yet also argue that the Soviets should play a major role in bringing the Vietnamese out of Kampuchea. Looked at from another angle, Gorbachev was only talking in Vladivostok about withdrawals and the engagements which it was *clearly* in the Soviet Union's power to embark upon because it was only *Soviet* troops involved; in this sense, Afghanistan, Mongolia and the Sino-Soviet border have throughout the 1980s been in a qualitatively different category from Kampuchea.

Thus the Vladivostok speech contained significant initiatives. Were these enough to placate the Chinese? The answer is that the Chinese acknowledged and welcomed what they perceived as some real change—certainly in the Soviet *statements* of policy—but were still cautious. Nevertheless, there have been some significant improvements in Sino-Soviet relations since mid-1986. In October 1986, the new chief Soviet negotiator in the Sino-Soviet negotiations, Rogachev, set another precedent by stating publicly that the USSR was now willing to discuss both the Afghanistan and the Kampuchea issues with China as part of the Sino-Soviet normalisation talks[36]; although this was *implicit* in the Vladivostok speech, the Soviets had not, apparently, openly acknowledged before that 'third party' issues could be discussed in the context of the bilateral negotiations.

We can now consider the actions, as distinct from the words, of the USSR on the three key issues.

On 15 January 1987, the Soviets announced that they would be withdrawing one motorised rifle division and various other military units from Mongolia by June of that year. According to Jarrett[37] this amounted to some 25 per cent of the Soviet military presence in Mongolia and thus represented a significant—if not massive—withdrawal. It appears to have been implemented. The Chinese certainly seem to have been satisfied with the direction of change, and have recently improved relations with Mongolia. In June 1987, for instance, a National People's Congress delegation spent a week in the PRM, and a boundary treaty—which outlines methods dealing with border disputes—was initialed in Ulan Bator.[38]

Since other chapters in this volume deal with the actualities of the Soviet withdrawal from Afghanistan, it is unnecessary to list the details again here. Suffice it to say that there have been actions as well as words. This said, the Chinese will continue to be wary for some time, whilst acknowledging that real improvements have taken place.

But what of the Indochina issue? 1988 witnessed what was in many ways the most significant change in Indochinese politics since 1979. For a variety of reasons, Hanoi declared at the end of May that it would shortly be announcing a total withdrawal of its troops from Kampuchea. Initially, there was some scepticism amongst outside observers; after all, Vietnam had made claims about troop 'withdrawals' on no fewer than six previous

133

occasions since 1982, and in the event these proved to be no more than troop rotations. But this time, withdrawal really seemed possible; there seemed to have been a *real* reduction of approximately 20000 troops late in 1987, and both the Soviet and the Vietnamese leaderships seemed more genuinely committed to withdrawal than ever before. The May 1988 statement claimed that there would be a net reduction of 50000 Vietnamese troops in Kampuchea by the end of 1988, and that *all* troops (an estimated further 50000-70000) would be out by the end of 1990. The withdrawal started within weeks, and initially proceeded far more rapidly than most observers had anticipated; very recent developments have led to some doubts that the 1988 target will be fully met, but it is not yet clear that the Vietnamese (or the Soviets) have fundamentally changed their position.[39]

It will by now be obvious that the USSR has in the last two years not only in word but also in deed made major advances in meeting the demands of the Chinese; it would be naive to argue that the USSR has taken these measures solely or even primarily to placate Beijing, but it is the case that the PRC now has much less reason not to engage in a serious improvement of relations with Moscow. Let us now consider the Chinese response to these developments.

As stated above, the Chinese do seem to have been pleased with the developments in Mongolia; this said, relatively little has been said on this issue recently.

The Chinese were initially very sceptical about the withdrawal from Afghanistan.[40] In February 1988, Acting Premier Li Peng told the visiting Pakistani Foreign Minister, Zain Noorani, that Soviet occupation of Afghanistan continued to be one of the key obstacles to improved Sino-Soviet relations and that China would wait and see whether or not the withdrawal would really proceed. There was still some scepticism after the signing of the Geneva Accords in April; however, the official Chinese response was to 'welcome' the signing of the accord, as a 'positive development' and to attribute it to the 'new thinking' in Soviet foreign policy. The Soviet announcement of June 1988 that they would withdraw all troops from the Wakhan Corridor by 15 August 1988 was also welcomed by the Chinese—who, however, would also have noted that the Soviets had declared they had trained 1200 Afghans to take over the operation of the (unspecified) facilities left in Badakhshan Province and the

Wakhan Corridor.[41] There is thus a lingering concern here for Beijing. Moreover, the Chinese continue to point to the difficulties there will be in reaching a political settlement, and are clearly far from believing that the Afghan problem is well on the way to a satisfactory solution.

The Chinese have recently been *linking* the Vietnamese occupation of Kampuchea explicitly with the Soviet occupation of Afghanistan. In an official statement from the Chinese Foreign Ministry of 1 July 1988, for instance, the point is made that 'the recent signing of the Geneva accords on a political settlement of the Afghan question has led to an even stronger demand by the international community for a prompt Vietnamese troop withdrawal from Kampuchea and for an early settlement of the Kampuchean question'.[42] There is, moreover, still considerable scepticism in the Chinese media about Vietnamese intentions.

Beyond the three obstacles

Although the Chinese have been emphasising the three obstacles in the 1980s, these are not the only factors that hinder or have hindered an improvement in Sino-Soviet relations. At this point it is appropriate to consider briefly some of the other factors, and the extent to which there have been recent changes relating to them.

1. *The Border Issue.* The territorial dispute between the USSR and the PRC is a complex and ancient one, with claims and counter-claims dating back at least to 1689, when the first treaty on the Sino-Russian frontier was signed.[43] An important aspect of the border dispute relates to the existence of a number of ethnic groups that straddle the border. In the past, it has often been assumed that each side was fearful that the other would encourage irredentist claims to the former's disadvantage. Recently, however, both Moscow and Beijing have had to deal with major surges in ethnic unrest—the Soviets in the Baltic regions, Kazakhstan, and Nagorno-Karabakh, the Chinese in Tibet and, in the last few months, Xinjiang. In my view, the Soviet and Chinese leaderships now have a common interest in not inciting nationalist unrest in the other's border regions, since both are aware of the possible knock-on effects of this. Moreover, the fact that both the Soviet and Chinese leaders are

experiencing some problems with, *inter alia*, Muslim nationalists not only means that they have a common problem but also that they must both have *some* reservations about the implications of the Soviet withdrawal from Afghanistan—even if the Chinese are unlikely to admit this publicly. As noted earlier, the Afghan resistance *might* inspire—directly or indirectly—anti-communist activity amongst Muslims in both the Soviet Central Asian republics and in various border regions of the PRC (notably Xinjiang); this is one reason why the present author believes that the Soviet occupation of the Wakhan Corridor has bothered the Chinese less than some Western commentators maintain.

2. *Leadership personality clashes.* There can be little doubt that personality clashes between Chinese and Soviet leaders have contributed to the souring of relations in the past. Zhao Ziyang is well aware that Gorbachev is very different from his predecessors, and there is to my knowledge no evidence that personal animosities between the two current General Secretaries are clouding Sino-Soviet relations or are likely to do so in the foreseeable future. This said, Deng's intransigence on the Vietnam issue might delay a further warming for a few months.

3. *Ideology.* Chinese attacks on Soviet revisionism and Soviet criticisms of Chinese dogmatism in the past reflected two aspects of ideology. The more obvious one is that there were radically different interpretations of the meaning of socialism, which to no small extent related to the two countries' different stages of economic development. Less obviously, the polemics reflected how seriously both sides—or at least the Chinese—treated ideology. Marxism-Leninism in its narrow sense was taken seriously.[44] By the 1980s, not only are the ideological perspectives of the two countries much closer—the slanging-match is over—but I would argue that classical Marxism-Leninism is much less important in both the USSR and the PRC. This is the era of the pragmatic communist and 'realistic' socialism. GDP clearly matters more than dialectical materialism. This is not to argue that *ideology* is less important—that would in my view represent a serious error of judgement. Rather, ideology is now far less concerned with a *telos*, and far more related to system—and particularly regime—legitimation. With the decline not only of differences in the vision but also in the significance of visions, there is now far less of a basis for ideological tensions

136

between the USSR and the PRC. Indeed, given the fears some Chinese leaders—even more than their Soviet counterparts—have of the pervasive influence of capitalist ideas within their own society, it might be the case that they will feel the need to side more than before with another 'Marxist-Leninist' state with similar policies in order to counter charges that they are abandoning their basic commitments.

4. *Cultural and Racial Tensions.* There is no question that racism and a poor understanding of each other's culture has played a role in Sino-Soviet tensions. The racism has tended to be more obvious amongst the Russians than the Chinese, and is well illustrated in Evtushenko's poem 'On the Red Snow of the Ussuri'; this said, the Soviets have on occasions accused the Chinese of having racist attitudes towards them.[45] But I would argue that this racism is a very minor factor in terms of the Sino-Soviet relationship. It is mostly a symbolic phenomenon, encouraged (or at least tolerated) by leaderships when it suits them because of more fundamental tensions in a relationship.

5. *Economic Interests.* The Chinese and the Soviets are adopting increasingly similar policies for economic development. The Chinese have translated Gorbachev's *Perestroika* into Mandarin, whilst the Soviets are now contemplating their first Special Economic Zone in Nakhodka. Chinese management methods are currently moving closer to the Soviet system, whilst the Soviets are learning from Chinese de-communisation and the family responsibility system. Both countries are encouraging private and cooperative enterprise. But the fact that the two countries are pursuing increasingly similar economic policies does not in itself imply that they will move closer. If we look at the *reasons* for the major changes in economic policy—basically, to make the economy perform better so as better to satisfy consumer demand, which in turn is geared to system and regime legitimation—then we begin to see more clearly a reason for an improvement in relations. This is that both sides are anxious to increase trade, and to exchange scientific and technological experience and knowledge. At present, the signs are that the recent marked increase in Sino-Soviet trade will continue, and there is no obvious reason why there should be a serious deterioration in Sino-Soviet relations because of economic and trade differences.

Conclusions

As stated at the beginning of this paper, the Afghanistan issue is not the major one in Sino-Soviet relations; whilst Soviet withdrawal will help the general atmosphere, it cannot be taken in isolation from the many other factors elaborated here. Although one must always be wary of speculation—the Chinese and/or Soviet leadership team could change, US foreign policy could move in a new direction, and so on—the bulk of the evidence does suggest that Sino-Soviet relations will continue to improve in the 1990s, whatever happens in Afghanistan. None the less, this relationship will never return to the imbalance of the 1950s; not only would China not accept this, but it is not clear to me that the Soviets are likely to want to return to that kind of relationship either. Rather, the relationship will be between more or less equal partners. Perhaps the greatest *symbol* of a major improvement would be a Sino-Soviet summit followed by a resumption of party-to-party—that is, CPSU and CPC—relations (these were severed in 1966); inter-party relations are more important in the communist world than inter-state relations.

In the past, some Western observers have suggested that a warmer relationship between Beijing and Moscow would constitute a threat to the West. Such thinking now seems to me to be outdated. It is extremely improbable that the Soviets and the Chinese will conjoin in a military alliance—unless, perhaps, the Japanese were to become far more of a military threat in the Far East than they have been.[46] Even then, I suspect that such an alliance would be limited and mostly of a symbolic nature. Moreover, the 'consumer imperative' in both the USSR and the PRC is now dominant, and is likely to remain so. Communism is not what it was. Stalin and Mao are dead, and the new communists know they have a lot to learn from capitalism. It is in this context that a continuing Sino-Soviet rapprochement should be seen.

FOOTNOTES

1   Gary Klintworth, 'Gorbachev's China Diplomacy', in Ramesh Thakur and Carlyle A. Thayer (eds.), *The Soviet Union as an Asian Pacific Power* (Boulder: Westview Press, 1987) pp.39-57, at p.46.

2   This section is a modified version of the analysis provided in Leslie Holmes, *Politics in the Communist World* (Oxford: Oxford University Press, 1986) pp.369-376.

3   *Beijing Review*, no.28, 1984, p.31 and no.5, 1988, p.9.

4   John W. Strong, 'The Sino-Soviet Dispute' in Adam Bromke and Teresa Rakowska-Harmstone (eds.), *The Communist States in Disarray 1965-1971* (Minneapolis: University of Minnesota Press, 1972) pp.21-42, at p.23.

5   For a useful survey of the ideological conflicts between China and the USSR in the late-1950s and early-1960s, plus many of the key documents, see Dieter Dux, *Ideology in Conflict: Communist Political Theory* (Princeton: Van Nostrand, 1963).

6   The series was published in *Peking Review*, no.17, 1960.

7   See, for example, Harrison Salisbury, *The Coming War Between Russia and China* (London: Secker and Warburg, 1969).

8   Adam Ulam, *Dangerous Relations: The Soviet Union in World Politics, 1970-1982* (New York: Oxford University Press, 1983) p.42.

9   See Henry Kissinger, *The White House Years* (Boston: Little Brown, 1979) p.886.

10   William E. Griffith, 'Sino-Soviet Rapprochement?', *Problems of Communism*, vol.32, no.2, March-April 1983, pp.20-29, at p.20.

11   *Pravda*, 25 March 1982, pp.1-2.

12   *The Twelfth National Congress of the CPC* (September 1982) (Beijing: Foreign Languages Press, 1982), p.56.

13   *Ibid.*, pp.58 and 59.

14   *Materialy XXVII s"ezda Kommunisticheskoi partii Sovetskogo Soiuza* (Moscow: Politizdat, 1986), p.72.

15   Gerald Segal, 'China and Afghanistan', *Asian Survey*, vol.21, no.11, November 1981, pp.1158-1174, at p.1161.

16   See *ibid.*, pp.1158-1159; Louis Dupree, *Afghanistan* (Princeton: Princeton University Press, 1980) p.424; J.R.V. Prescott, *Map of Mainland Asia by Treaty* (Melbourne: Melbourne University Press, 1975) pp.137-140.

17   J.Bruce Amstutz, *Afghanistan: The First Five Years of Soviet Occupation* (Washington: National Defense University Press, 1986) p.294.

18   *Ibid.*, p.295; Desmond Ball, *Soviet Signals Intelligence (SIGINT): The Ground Stations and Systems* (Canberra: Reference Paper No. 139, Strategic and Defence Studies Centre, Research School of Pacific Studies, Australian National University, April 1986) p.22.

19   Amstutz, *op.cit.*, p.296.

20 Amstutz, *ibid.*, p.296, states that the Chinese declared the new agreement invalid in July 1981, but cites only Western sources to support his claim; Segal, *loc. cit.*, p.1160, claims there was no Chinese comment.

21 Amstutz, *op.cit.*, p.298.

22 Gerald Segal, 'Sino-Soviet relations: the new agenda', *The World Today*, vol.44, no.6, June 1988, pp.95-99, at p.97.

23 On all this see John G. Merriam, 'Arms Shipments to the Afghan Resistance', in Grant M. Farr and John G. Merriam (eds.), *Afghan Resistance: The Politics of Survival* (Boulder: Westview Press, 1987) pp.71-101.

24 See Yaacov Vertzberger, 'Afghanistan in China's Policy', *Problems of Communism*, vol.31, no.3, May-June 1982, pp.1-23, at pp.9-12; and Amstutz, *op.cit.*, p.295.

25 *Ibid.*, p.295.

26 Anthony Hyman, *Afghanistan Under Soviet Domination 1964-83* (London: Macmillan, 1984) p.125.

27 *Ibid.*, pp.59, 142.

28 *Ibid.*, pp.141-142.

29 *Ibid.*, p.142.

30 However, despite Chinese attitudes towards Pol Pot, the latter was not as pro-Chinese as is sometimes assumed. For a statement (August 16 1988) by Zhao Ziyang that the precondition for high-level Sino-Soviet talks is that the USSR must urge Vietnam to withdraw from Kampuchea see *Beijing Review*, no.37, 1988, p.7.

31 'Text of Speech by Mikhail Gorbachev in Vladivostok, 28 July 1986' in Thakur and Thayer, *op.cit.*, pp.201-227, at p.219.

32 *Ibid.*, p.224.

33 *Ibid.*, p.225.

34 *Materialy XXVII s" ezda Kommunisticheskoi partii Sovetskogo Soiuza* (Moscow: Politizdat, 1986), p.69.

35 'Text of Speech by Mikhail Gorbachev in Vladivostok, 28 July 1986', *loc. cit.*, p.223.

36 Klintworth, *loc. cit.*, p.40.

37 Kenneth Jarrett, 'Mongolia in 1987: Out From the Cold?', *Asian Survey*, vol.28, no.1, January 1988, pp.78-85, at p.81.

38 See *ibid.*, pp.80-81 and *Far Eastern Economic Review*, 9 July 1987, pp.24-5.

39 See *The Age*, 27 June 1988 and 19 September 1988.

40 See *Beijing Review*, no.2, 1988, p.10 and no.9, 1988, p.10.

41 See *Beijing Review*, no.17, 1988, pp.9-10; *Renmin Ribao*, 17 April 1988 in BBC *Summary of World Broadcasts* FE/0131/C/2-3, 21 April 1988; and *Xinhua*, 29 June 1988 in BBC *Summary of World Broadcasts* FE/0192/C/3, 1 July 1988.

42 *Beijing Review*, no.28, 1988, pp.6-7.

43 For a scholarly survey of both this treaty, and subsequent treaties and negotiations on the Russian-Chinese border, see Prescott, *op.cit.*, pp.5-89.

44 On the distinction between 'narrow' and 'broad' conceptions of Marxism-Leninism, see Holmes, *op.cit.*, especially pp.99, 114.
45 See, for example, *Pravda*, 14 July 1963, p.1.
46 For a concise, up-to-date analysis of the development of Japan's defence—and defence industries—see Ron Matthews and Joanne Bartlett, 'The Stirring of Japan's Military Slumber', *The World Today*, vol.44, no.5, May 1988, pp.79-82.

9

The Afghanistan 'Settlement' and the Future of World Politics

Richard A. Falk

It is important to realise that Soviet withdrawal should not be confused with the attainment of real peace and justice in Afghanistan, that the war there is far from over, and that the responsibilities of those governments and private initiatives that have helped the Afghan people are now in a new phase, and have certainly not ended. In my view, we need to remind ourselves of this reality. Otherwise, it is likely that our attention will lapse, and that our political leaders and media will unwittingly facilitate our forgetting Afghanistan.

In many respects, I feel that few situations since the Second World War have so challenged the moral and political resources of the West as has the Soviet invasion of Afghanistan. Especially for those who, like myself, have been critical over the years of US interventionary diplomacy in the Third World it sometimes seemed difficult to encourage support for the Afghan resistance in the face of the perception that much of the official level of outrage about the Soviet invasion in our countries seemed opportunistic, a way of reviving Cold War tensions to justify increases in arms spending and the like. Despite such complicating circumstances the Afghan ordeal has been above all a challenge to those of us who believe in the rights of the peoples of the world to control their political, economic, and cultural destiny free from outside military and paramilitary interference.

In this chapter, I propose to consider the international implications of the Soviet withdrawal. This emphasis relieves me of the obligation to consider either the unfolding of the struggle within Afghanistan or the regional effects of Soviet withdrawal. Fortunately, others in this volume have taken on these related concerns. I do this while trying at the same time to insist that Soviet withdrawal cannot be separated altogether from other aspects of the continuing Afghan struggle for self-determination.

My sense of 'international implications' is, perhaps, overly associated with the Geneva Accords of April 1988 that have established the regional international parameters of Soviet withdrawal. My focus on the Geneva Accords expresses an anxiety that reflects my earlier preoccupation with the Vietnam peace process that culminated in the Paris Accords of 1973, a set of agreements that facilitated US withdrawal but in a manner exacting a high and continuing cost from the Vietnamese people. It was not only that those Paris agreements were themselves flawed, but that their implementation turned out to be irresponsible and destructive on all sides. I believe we must work hard to ensure that such a pattern is not also the fate of the Geneva Accords of 1988.

A final introductory observation bears directly on these agreements. On their face, key provisions of these agreements can be interpreted in several ways, and it is important that our primary understanding be associated with their main objective— to facilitate the struggle of the Afghan people for self-determination. To me, this implies continuing support for the Afghan resistance. No literalist or legalist reading of these Geneva Accords should be allowed to stand in the way of assuring the political completion of the resistance victory. Of course, the form of such support should itself be mindful of sustaining Soviet disengagement from Afghanistan: it is important to resist the temptation to be provocative; and to avoid providing pretexts for Moscow to reverse this process.

In discussing Soviet withdrawal from Afghanistan, we encounter familiar problems associated with interpreting 'effects' at the level of international relations. Causal connections are, at best, speculative. At most, one can generalise that the Soviet Union's willingness to withdraw its troops rapidly is likely to encourage, at least and, perhaps, only in the short run, those forces in both superpowers that seek more moderate East-West relations. Without an overt Soviet military role in Afghanistan, almost no matter what else should happen there, the US-Soviet relationship could continue to improve. In this regard, Soviet withdrawal from Afghanistan is consistent with the overall thrust of Gorbachev's leadership as embodied especially in the proceedings of the historic 27th Congress of the Soviet Communist Party—namely, according priority to *perestroika*; reducing East-West tensions; and eliminating by unilateral initiative expensive and unsuccessful Soviet commitments overseas, especially in the Third World.

On the basis of this kind of now widely shared consensus, it is possible to pronounce somewhat more specifically on the likely international implications of the expected Soviet withdrawal. To underscore a qualification already suggested, Soviet withdrawal from Afghanistan is internationally significant because it adds to a pre-existing momentum toward more positive East-West relations and represents a further step in a determined Soviet effort to make a series of adjustments in its foreign policy, both to overcome a sense of geopolitical overextension and to take account of an intense, if provisional, process of internal self-criticism that repudiates virtually all aspects of Brezhnev era foreign policy.

Despite this tone of confident and positive expectation arising from the Soviet withdrawal from Afghanistan, a central uncertainty exists with regard to international effects arising from the unpredictability at this stage of the United States response and the Soviet reaction to this response. Depending on this interplay, widely divergent results could flow from the geopolitical end-game in Afghanistan. The Soviet turn inwards could be interpreted in Washington either as a call to relax on the international level and recognise an unsurpassed opportunity to redress US overextension in a parallel fashion or, alternatively, it could be construed as an unprecedented 'opening' to push ahead with the spread of Western values, as well as to deliver a knockout blow to godless Communism, enabling the United States to fulfill Henry Luce's vision of 'an American century.'

Both patterns of response enjoy considerable support within United States leadership circles, and the public could be swayed either way at this stage. The geopolitical dynamic flowing from either scenario is highly unstable, but a first approximation would suppose that US reciprocation, that is, US corresponding moves to the Soviet withdrawal, would encourage and reinforce the current 'new thinking' in the Kremlin, whereas US assertiveness in the face of perceived Soviet weakness would likely produce a backlash in Moscow, either to preserve Gorbachev's credibility or as an instrument in the hands of a neo-Stalinist opposition that lies in waiting throughout the Soviet bureaucracy to ambush Gorbachev's approach to the future should an opportunity present itself.

Let us entertain one line of speculation. Although it could not be demonstrated or proven, and would never be acknowledged by Soviet leaders (especially if correct), from the outset of Soviet aggression against Afghanistan in late 1979, I had a strong intuitive feeling that especially the opposition in Poland, and more generally in Eastern Europe, would be rewarded by a measure of Soviet forbearance—in effect, that Soviet leaders would be strongly inhibited from unleashing the international consequences of undertaking a second military intervention beyond their borders. Carrying this geopolitical reasoning a further step, again without any hard supporting evidence, one could argue that the disposition by the United States to intervene against the perceived spread of Soviet influence in Central America was strengthened by the invasion of Afghanistan. Thus, distant but lethal international implications of the Soviet invasion, to a degree, insulated Poland and exposed Nicaragua to superpower intervention.

Can we not, then, raise the opposite sequence of possibilities in the post-withdrawal setting of superpower policy? Might not the Soviet Union feel increased pressure to arrest its sense of decline, if the withdrawal from Afghanistan is followed by a surge of anti-Soviet militancy in Eastern Europe? And, contrariwise, might not the perception of the Soviets ignominiously withdrawing from a country on their central Asian borders diminish the credibility of claiming that Soviet strategic expansion underlies revolutionary nationalism in countries like Nicaragua and El Salvador?

145

Perhaps to an unprecedented extent, the struggle of the Afghan resistance received support from world public opinion. As long as the Soviet interventionary presence was prominent, this pressure ensured that cynical political leaders in the West would not 'forget' Afghanistan. Effective opposition to Soviet intervention in Afghanistan is properly viewed, I believe, as one of the few genuine triumphs of President Reagan's foreign policy approach. If taken on its own, it could even provide some validation for the Reagan Doctrine of lending support to anti-Communist resistance struggles. But, of course, it cannot be taken on its own. The circumstances in Afghanistan that justified lending international military and economic support to the resistance were dominated by the facts of massive, prior Soviet military intervention. The case for aid to the resistance, then, was consistent with support for Afghan rights of self-determination, and arguably, in light of the Soviet intervention, such aid was an indispensable contribution to the realisation of these rights. In contrast, consider the situation in Nicaragua. There, support for the Contras seems on its face to be an effort to rupture a course of self-determination in Nicaragua that produced a result that was objectionable to Washington. Given the US effort to reverse the political process in Nicaragua, including through reliance on covert operations and paramilitary tactics, the provision of Cuban and Soviet aid to the Sandinista government seems appropriate, and in the context, supportive of the overall process of self-determination. In each situation of alleged intervention, the facts must be interpreted to assess competing claims. On this basis, I believe that most independent observers would share both of my conclusions: namely, that helping the Afghan resistance has been a contribution to self-determination, whereas helping the Contras is an obstruction to self-determination.

Putting aside the merits of earlier United States and international support, the paramount policy concern now becomes whether once the galvanising presence of overt Soviet intervention is removed, the world will once again 'forget' Afghanistan while the unfinished business of the war remains. There are a number of elements that constitute this unfinished business: it is possible that other forms of Soviet intervention can remain or even increase, as troops are withdrawn; the future of more than five million Afghan refugees living in Pakistan and

146

Iran remains clouded; but most important of all, the horrifying legacy of superpower intervention could make an Afghan 'peace' as ghastly in its way as has been the terrible ordeal of war. This horrifying legacy consists of a disrupted political, economic, cultural, and social order, as well as the more literal residue of the war itself in the form of millions of unexploded land mines, vast arsenals of military equipment, and a variety of covert operations. Such problems of post-withdrawal Afghanistan need to be addressed in the difficult setting of persisting civil strife and likely efforts by regional powers, especially India and Pakistan, to exert control over Afghanistan's future. The point here is that the effects of the superpower role in Afghanistan's internal affairs during the past decade cannot be nullified by the Soviet withdrawal, even if it follows the Geneva scheme to the letter. The responsibility of the superpowers, especially of the Soviet Union, cannot so easily be discharged. At the same time, it is important to be confident that the banner of a continuing responsibility does not serve as a new pretext for further intervention. The question of the nature and appropriate implementation of Soviet post-withdrawal responsibility is delicate and, as far as I know, almost completely unexamined.

At the same time, the actuality of the Soviet withdrawal process is a momentous achievement attributable in large part to international pressures brought to bear on Moscow. Removing the Soviet military presence from Afghanistan was the most important single step that could be taken in the direction of self-determination. What is more, that this process was to be completed within a nine month period delayed the internal process of struggle no more than was necessary under the circumstances. To have realised these results through international negotiations was an impressive achievement of the Geneva Accords of 1988, but it should not be confused with bringing 'peace' or 'justice' to Afghanistan. While appreciating the Geneva Accords, it is also important to acknowledge their limitations. These limitations are as pertinent to the prospects of international implications as are the more apparent benefits of the agreements.

In considering international implications it is helpful, if discouraging, to keep in mind a comparison with the ending of the American involvement in Vietnam. I do not want to re-argue the case on the American involvement, a subject that remains

147

volatile sixteen years after the US role ended, but simply to point out that the positive international implications associated with the settlement quickly evaporated when the internal order in Vietnam collapsed in a chaotic and, for Washington, humiliating fashion. Indeed, the long shadow of the Paris Accords of 1973 that ended the US military presence in Vietnam is cast upon our sense of the Geneva Accords of 1988. The Paris Accords, as is well known, did not bring peace and justice to Vietnam (nor did the earlier 1954 Geneva Accords that ended the French colonial war), although they did enable self-determination and led to a process that brought the internal war to an end within two years. The double message here is this: the Afghanistan settlement of 1988 was an indispensable step forward, but it provided no assurance either that the ordeal of Afghan society would come to a satisfactory conclusion or that it was appropriate for outside actors to wash their hands of the situation in Afghanistan and turn to other matters. Thus, when it comes to 'international implications', it is inappropriate to suppose that the Geneva Accords have done more than promise the removal of the irritant of the Soviet military intervention. The immediate fallout of removing this irritant is sure to promote a constructive overall atmosphere in international relations, but the possibility of a longer-term positive influence depends significantly on how the unfinished international agenda on Afghanistan is handled by the major outside actors.

With these considerations in the background, it becomes possible to reach more concrete conclusions about the wider international implications of the Soviet withdrawal. These implications can be discussed by reference to several distinct topics: (a) implications for Soviet foreign policy; (b) implications for East-West and superpower relations, including US foreign policy; (c) implications for the dynamics of self-determination elsewhere in the Third World; (d) implications for the future of world order. Treating these topics as distinct is analytically convenient, but admittedly artificial. These clusters of implications do not form distinct categories, but rather provide, at best, organising concepts with fluid and shifting boundaries. The interactions among these categories may be, in the end, as significant as what seems to occur within each.

On Soviet Foreign Policy

The impact of the withdrawal in Moscow should be initially understood as part of a broader and seemingly fundamental reorientation of all aspects of Soviet domestic and foreign policy. If indeed Gorbachev is a second Lenin, the ridding from Soviet foreign policy of its Afghanistan millstone is of great substantive and symbolic importance, especially enabling Soviet leaders to propose constructive initiatives in other areas of international life with far greater credibility.

A provisional result of the withdrawal from Afghanistan will be to signal an overall withdrawal of the Soviet Union from active engagement more generally in the Third World. By this, I do not mean a dramatic abandonment by Moscow of existing commitments, especially to countries such as Cuba and Ethiopia with avowed Marxist-Leninist orientations. Rather, what seems in the offing is a far more constructive Soviet attitude toward the peaceful resolution of regional conflicts, and a greater reluctance by Moscow to take on new commitments in the future on behalf of resistance and liberation movements. In effect, it seems likely that 'the lesson of Afghanistan' for the current generation of Soviet leaders is to avoid, if at all possible, any further military involvements in the Third World; and to do this effectively will probably require a downgrading of bilateral diplomacy and an upgrading of multilateral approaches. Such a lesson seems likely to exert a comparably greater influence on Soviet leaders than the significantly corresponding experience of Vietnam did upon American leaders. For one thing, the Soviet leadership has itself acknowledged failure in Afghanistan to a much clearer extent and seems to have been united on the importance of rapid withdrawal.

Of course, one should not push this matter of Soviet acknowledgment too far or too unreservedly. As recently as Gorbachev's publication of *Perestroika*, the Soviet position in Afghanistan is rationalised and defended, with the United States being held responsible for covertly organising the breakdown of order and prolonging civil strife. If the post-withdrawal process goes badly, the Soviet leadership could be expected to revive its claims that Washington, not Moscow, was the culprit all along.[1] In contrast, the pro-interventionary forces in Vietnam have not until this day acknowledged defeat in Vietnam. Many believe that the American effort was on the verge of victory when disrupted by domestic US developments—the loss of political will by the public and the politicians, as well as a misinterpretation of the battlefield experience. This viewpoint generally rests on an interpretation of the Tet Offensive as a desperate gamble and a shattering military defeat for Hanoi, rather than as stunning demonstration that Washington's claims to be winning were either based on illusions or deceit. In contrasting the Soviet reaction to its Afghan pullout with the US reaction to its Vietnam pullout, it is important to understand that at no point did the American public repudiate. This reality was somewhat disguised because a large number of Americans who in the months after the Tet Offensive preferred escalation to withdrawal came to regard rapid withdrawal as preferable to continued persistence in the Vietnam quagmire as a consequence of Johnson's 'no-win' strategy. Recent public opinion research has shown, for instance, that a majority of Eugene McCarthy's supporters in the early 1968 presidential primaries whose results so shocked Lyndon Johnson's White House, were actually hawkish opponents of the then current approach, who have remained to this day ardent supporters of the underlying interventionary mission on behalf of the Saigon regime. Even without this degree of ambiguity, it seems evident that part of Ronald Reagan's extraordinary voter popularity was based on his successful attack on US foreign policy in the post-Vietnam period as lacking the resolve to uphold US interests and pride in the Third World by military force. Reaganism was, in part, a reaction to the American experience of humiliation, symbolised by the chaotic departure from the roof of its Saigon Embassy and by the long captivity of its diplomats in Teheran in the embassy seizure in November 1979 by radical elements in the Iranian Revolution.

At present, the impression is that the Soviet withdrawal from Afghanistan is a genuine turning-point in Moscow's foreign policy. This impression is reinforced powerfully by the apparent priority placed by the Gorbachev leadership upon domestic reform, the whole spirit of which is captured by the repeated incantation of such words as *perestroika* and *glasnost'*, a terminology that lacks any roots in the Marxist-Leninist lexicon. Such an emphasis could easily develop into consistent support for self-determination, and an acknowledgment that intervention does not work. But what if the United States were to continue to intervene, not on behalf of self-determination, but to block it? What would the Gorbachev leadership (or its internal opposition) do if it began to perceive conflict situations as being shaped by an unopposed United States Government being offered a blank cheque or a world order bargain by this turn inward by the Soviet Union? Might the Soviets reverse directions, just as the Americans did after 1979, if their current approach comes to be regarded as a failure?

The orbit of speculation of international effects can be narrowed to the specific consequences for Afghanistan that follow upon Soviet withdrawal. If Soviet withdrawal produces a humiliation for the Kremlin then the continuation of that process could be drawn into question. For instance, if either a bloody purge of those Afghans who had sided with communism and supported the Soviet role in the country occurs or if withdrawal leads to a geopolitical reversal in which a new Afghan leadership becomes formally aligned itself with the United States, it might discredit the Soviet advocates of rapid withdrawal. Some reckoning for the crimes of state committed on behalf of Soviet puppet regimes in Kabul during the past decade will probably figure prominently on the agenda of a new government that represents the various strands of the resistance movement. At minimum, one can expect a fresh stream of refugees generated by the new political order leaving Afghanistan in fear, and quite possibly unwelcome anywhere, even including the Soviet Union. It is also entirely plausible that an internal rivalry for control of the political process in Afghanistan will produce a variety of manifestations of militant anti-Soviet attitudes, not unlike the 1979 takeover of the US Embassy in Teheran during the first phases of Khomeini rule in Iran in which radical elements were seeking to discredit the more moderate elements of the revolution that were still in control of the governmental structure. That is, the internal struggle of Afghanistan to claim rights of national leadership may be waged according to which factions in the resistance most successfully project an image of undiluted anti-Sovietism. Depending on how *perestroika* is proceeding, on the character of the internal opposition in Moscow, on US policy, and on the perception of Soviet decline, current expectations about Soviet withdrawal from Third World turmoil might have to be abruptly revised.

Short of such developments, what are the expectations flowing from the Soviet withdrawal? Perhaps the most likely effect, already upon us, is active Soviet support for the rapid resolution of regional conflicts, especially those with an East-West dimension, along negotiable lines—the so-called 'season of peace' that has included the Iran-Iraq ceasefire, the southern African agreement on Angola and Namibia, and that has witnessed diplomatic movement on facilitating Vietnamese withdrawal from Kampuchea. These developments are properly associated with an international mood largely established by Soviet withdrawal from Afghanistan, although specific causal links are denied and cannot be established. In this regard, the new Soviet diplomacy can be associated with a strong endorsement of peaceful settlement procedures, and more surprisingly, with attempts to entrust the United Nations with a central role in all phases of the settlement process.

Let us revert once more to a comparison with Vietnam. It is unthinkable that the United States would have allowed the Secretariat of the United Nations to play anything like the mediating role that it has played and will continue to play over Afghanistan. Surely the United Nations is not a friendly arena for Soviet policy on Afghanistan. To accept this United Nations role, then, is to take a calculated risk that the Soviet objections will fall on deaf ears during the withdrawal process. No one could imagine Washington accepting such a prospect at this stage, say, in relation to a Central American peace process— and this despite the far less focused objections to the United States role than to the Soviet presence in Afghanistan.

A second set of expectations, perhaps not deliberately orchestrated by the Kremlin, would induce radical political forces in ongoing struggles around the world to compromise their objectives or even to avoid confrontation, partly because they could not count on any assured level of Soviet support. One imagines that the Sandinistas view the Soviet withdrawal from Afghanistan as a further signal from Moscow not to expect too much support, and possibly to confront the prospect of a virtual geopolitical abandonment. Possibly, such a signal will be offset by other contrary developments, including the weaknesses of the Contras, an increased commitment by Cuba (Castro has been openly critical of Gorbachev's foreign policy), shifts in American foreign policy as a result of the 1988 US presidential election, and a growing Latin American opposition to continued US intervention. Similarly, one can understand Soviet moves in the direction of promoting an Arab-Israeli settlement. The recent Soviet willingness to reestablish diplomatic ties with Israel and their relatively low profile opposition to Israeli practices in the Occupied Territories during the *intifada* can be read as expressions of new timidity in international relations and as a diplomatic repositioning to enable a more genuine contribution by the USSR to a future peace process in the region.

On Superpower and East-West Relations, and Some Implications for US Foreign Policy

Turning from Third World revolutionary nationalism to East-West relations, generally, one would expect the Afghanistan withdrawal to aid those forces on both sides that favour a moderate international order that puts the new *détente* on a solid footing and could even achieve a dramatic muting of the Cold War, if not its actual end. This latter goal largely depends on developments in Europe, especially whether the Kremlin is prepared to yield in Eastern Europe to the various societal forces of self-determination that are demanding human rights and democracy, including, at the very least, an insistence on protecting sovereign rights against Soviet hegemonic claims; to maintain the Gorbachev momentum will require an acceptance by Moscow of far looser forms of control over Eastern European countries. Possibly, a series of linked arrangements resembling Finlandisation might be imagined to grow up in place of the tight control and bloc cohesiveness of the Warsaw Pact.

The Afghanistan withdrawal is not causative as much as it is symptomatic of broader tendencies. The acknowledgment by both superpowers of a need for adjustments in foreign policy as a consequence of geopolitical overextension is the decisive structural element here. Important, also, is the failure of Soviet efforts to legitimate the regimes that hold power in Eastern Europe. After more than four decades, an occupying Soviet Army, a record of periodic bloody interventions at times of crisis, and a continuous threat of renewed intervention have been relied upon by Moscow to uphold the *status quo*. Gorbachev has shown signs of admitting these realities, and of searching for a new European policy that would include the willingness to relax the Soviet grip on Eastern Europe. If this diplomacy goes forward, it will be difficult to retain for very long *any* foreign military forces in Europe, and the East-West conflict will either disappear or renew itself in a very different form, most likely as a standoff between the two halves of Europe. In most reading of postwar history, the Cold War was essentially about the unresolved character of European arrangements, a condition typified by the absence of any European peace treaty. If new arrangements become acceptable to both superpowers, then it will be hard to sustain the credibility of their rivalry, even though some political forces on both sides, but especially on the Western side, will be reluctant to let go of an ideological interpretation of contemporary geopolitics. This prospect may be deferred or avoided, however, if Western European economic integration leads to a simultaneous process of diplomatic decoupling from the United States and regional militarisation that includes Franco-German-British cooperation leading to a joint nuclear weapons policy.

Short of this, Soviet initiatives in the arms control area are likely to go forward and obtain considerable public backing, including in the United States and Europe. Already, American conservatives are arguing that Gorbachev has discovered how easy it is to gain diplomatic credit and geopolitical advantage simply by accepting US negotiating proposals, as was largely the case in relation to the INF treaty. Their claim is that US arms control positions even in the Reagan era were public relations postures premised on the view that they were 'safe' because one could count on Moscow to reject them. Now, however, the United States must, according to this view, not get tricked in the future. Such a polemic, although surely touching a raw nerve, is also rather absurd. Had INF obligations been reversed, it is inconceivable that an American president could have survived endorsing an agreement that calls for the United States to dismantle three times as many nuclear warheads as the Soviet Union!

As far as future negotiations are concerned, they will be based on overall national security policy by both superpowers. Moscow has already displayed a willingness to move in the direction of a world without nuclear weapons, and seems prepared to do so in virtually any manner acceptable to Washington. Such a willingness has produced a split in Washington; first, the hawk position stresses American dependence on a nuclear option, given its inferiority in conventional forces and its long supply lines to some areas of vital interest (for example the Persian Gulf). This position seeks to retain the nuclear arsenal, even to augment it, regardless of what the Soviets propose. Second, the centrist position that is guiding most liberals is receptive to various modest denuclearising possibilities so long as the underlying nuclear capability called for by 'deterrence', including 'extended deterrence', is not eroded. That is, arms control in certain forms is favoured, but there are limits, as well, that derive from the nature of the states system rather than from a reading as to whether or not to rely upon Gorbachev's sincerity. This liberal position might be marginally more receptive to some of those of Gorbachev's initiatives that do not look toward the complete elimination of nuclear weapons from the scene, but could have greater difficulty gaining a domestic consensus in Congress. Negotiations on these matters is made politically easier by the Soviet withdrawal from Afghanistan, but the substance of what is agreed upon will depend on quite independent assessments of national interests, as well as on the play of party politics on the American side. These assessments will be influenced by a deep bureaucratic attachment by the national security establishment to nuclear weaponry and by a reactionary strain of public opinion that sees virtually all constraints on military power as undesirable interferences with the sovereign rights of a great power.

On Intervention, Self-Determination, and Third World Nationalism

The Soviet withdrawal from Afghanistan contributes one more precedent on behalf of the capacity of revolutionary nationalist forces to prevail in the end against a massive interventionary force and triumph over seemingly insuperable odds. Expressed differently, the Soviet defeat in Afghanistan strengthens the argument against superpower intervention in the Third World, and opens the way toward greater self-determination for small countries. The dynamics of self-determination do not necessarily produce political climates favourable to human rights and

155

democracy, as the outcome of the Iranian Revolution has so vividly illustrated. Living with Third World nationalisms may actually strengthen certain forms of political extremism, especially fundamentalist forces.

Much depends on whether the superpowers (and others) can translate their recent frustrations as intervenors into meaningful codes of international conduct, including restrictions on the supply of arms. On the American side, attitudes remain ambivalent and polarised. Many conservatives regard the Soviet withdrawal from Afghanistan as one more demonstration of the success of a diplomacy of force, and as a successful application of the Reagan Doctrine, that is, as coerced by Stinger missiles and support for the *Mujahideen* rather than reflecting a change of heart in the Kremlin. To the extent this view prevails—and it has been embodied in the important Pentagon report entitled *Discriminate Deterrence* and is a tenet of George Bush's worldview—selective military intervention on the anti-Marxist side in Third World arenas remains a workable, beneficial policy. Reliance on the Reagan Doctrine was compatible with indigenous nationalism in Afghanistan, but it seems to work against it in other areas of preferred application such as Central America and southern Africa. At this stage, the eventual impacts of the Soviet withdrawal from Afghanistan remain difficult to assess.

At the same time, if the superpowers begin relinquishing their interventionary roles in the Third World, it is likely to work to the advantage of international law and the United Nations. Indeed, without superpower involvement, especially if ideological rivalry is muted and cooperation becomes possible over a wider range of regional issues, then the UN (or regional institutions) provide an attractive alternative, in some instances, to chaos and persisting bloodshed. One definite consequence of generalising the current Soviet posture of withdrawal from overseas commitments is to draw into greater question the viability of superpower spheres of influence as stabilising (and repressive) elements in the overall structure on international order. Whether new political actors in the wake of the loosening, or even disintegration, of hegemonic blocs, succeed in creating spheres of influence of their own is one uncertainty about the near future of international relations.

If, indeed, Soviet withdrawal can be understood as part of a wider process of adjustment to a multi-polar world, it is quite sure that dominant states in various regions will seek to expand their own geopolitical roles, and perhaps stimulate new rivalries, leading even to new patterns of warfare. The Iran-Iraq War, although a consequence of many developments, can also be seen as a regional war to determine relative status in a circumstance of geopolitical confusion, given the collapse of colonialism and the fall of the Shah's regime in Iran. It is not impossible that before the Afghan ferment is resolved, it will provoke a regional hegemonic war. My argument boils down to this: Soviet withdrawal from Afghanistan, and more generally, superpower deference to Third World nationalism is desirable on its face, but it may have the deferred disturbing implication of generating a new type of regional warfare fought with highly destructive, modern weaponry.

World Order Implications

An inconclusive note on the wider international implications of the Afghanistan settlement seems unavoidable at this stage. The final settlement depends on too many factors moving in contradictory directions, and the framework of obligations established at Geneva can be construed in a variety of ways.

Let me conclude with two rather divergent judgments. First a discouraging one: as with other East-West conflicts in the Third World, the outcome in Afghanistan reaffirms *the primacy of geopolitics*. Little care at Geneva was devoted to finding transitional political arrangements that would reduce subsequent risks of deadly civil strife throughout Afghanistan without impairing the unfolding of self-determination. After years of superpower rivalry, Afghanistan is seemingly being set adrift, as much of an abstraction in relation to a prospect of 'peace' as it had been a geopolitical battleground during a time of 'war'. The dominant hypocrisy of the anti-Soviet diplomacy in the West is starkly exposed as indifference to the well-being of the people of Afghanistan. I would not deny that a circumstance of tragedy is inevitably created by prolonged military intervention, but a termination of that intervention in a way that seems indifferent to the fate of the population is only marginally preferable to the

157

intervention itself. In fact, on a more general level such abstract geopolitics represents a continuation of the refusal to be influenced in international policy-making by the concrete realities of human suffering.

On the positive side is the further demonstration, largely attributable to the strength and versatility of Afghan resistance, of the *primacy of politics* in the resolution of internal conflict. Such a conclusion reverses the still reigning conventional wisdom that military force dominates politics, and that military advantages overwhelm other factors in deep encounters of opposed political forces. The events in Afghanistan, as earlier in Vietnam and elsewhere, suggest that gaining the military upper hand in a weaker foreign country, in the absence of holding the right political cards, raises the levels of firepower, destruction, and casualties, but does not provide control over the outcome. These struggles for political supremacy in this historical period seem resolved more by the side that most successfully commands symbols of national legitimacy, especially those that affirm traditional cultural values and that emphasise the autonomy of the nationalist polity (as against a willed or imposed dependence on foreign powers). The detribalised urban regime in Kabul was in no position to contest these symbols of legitimacy even without taking account of its discrediting subordination to Moscow. In some respects, subordination to Moscow followed from the inability of this kind of the Afghan Marxist leadership to satisfy nationalist expectations. As the outcomes in Cuba, Vietnam, Nicaragua suggest, a Marxist leadership can compete successfully for these nationalist symbols under certain conditions. The main conclusion, however, is that the legitimacy of a political movement depends on its successful appropriation of the symbols of nationalism, and that this success can compensate for economic and military vulnerability. Further, it appears that superior resources and weaponry are difficult to bring successfully to bear unless the legitimacy struggle can be won, or at least stalemated.

This potency of nationalism also reinforces other indications of great power military disability, including the self-destructive character of general warfare and the economic drain associated with an indefinite process of preparing for war as the main foundation of national security, including the diversion of scientific and engineering talents away from civilian priorities. To compete successfully in the world economy of the next century may induce the major states in the world to consider seriously for the first time a process that dismantles by stages the war system. If so, it is likely that the Vietnam and Afghanistan outcomes will be regarded as significant contributions to this Second Enlightenment.

Conclusions

Before finishing, I would like to recover a sense of moral centre in the unresolved torment of Afghanistan. In this spirit, two broad sets of challenges unfold from the Geneva Accords and the dynamics of Soviet withdrawal. First is the overall discrediting of interventionary diplomacy in the Third World, and more generally, the reinforcement of the declining utility of military superiority in international relations; as such, the outcome in Afghanistan points to the desirability of exploring other approaches to international order, including an enhanced role for regional actors and the United Nations. Second is the difficulty of balancing considerations favourable to respect for rights of self-determination of peoples against procedures of accountability (Soviet Union) and policies of responsibility (USA) in relation to Afghan tragedies associated with wartime devastation, persisting civil strife, and social reconstruction; the proper international role remains deeper and wider than blunting patterns of geopolitical encroaching—that is, conducting the East-West rivalry on blood-soaked Third World 'playing fields'.[2]

There is here at this stage in the Afghanistan struggle an important test of remembering and forgetting. How well this test is passed will shape whether we look back on Geneva '88 as an opportunistic disgrace or as a positive milestone. The millions of unexploded mines that lie buried throughout the Afghan countryside and that will imperil civilian life for decades to come, serve us well as a metaphor of the yet unresolved destiny of Afghanistan, as well as a reminder that until those mines are safely removed outsiders continue to bear a responsibility for what goes on within Afghanistan.

With an eye on the prospect of Soviet withdrawal, Ronald Reagan issued a Presidential proclamation declaring March 21, 1988 to be Afghanistan Day. This statement has been mainly quoted to support the view that the Geneva pledge of non-intervention should be interpreted on the basis of symmetry rather than to allow continuing Soviet support for the Kabul regime to stand on a different plane than help to the Afghan *Mujahideen*. In closing I would like to quote from another passage in the Proclamation: 'Our commitment to the freedom of the Afghan people will not end should the Soviets withdraw. We will join other nations and international organisations to help the Afghans rebuild their country and their institutions ... The United States has consistently supported the Afghans in their long ordeal. That support will continue. We will rejoice with them when true peace is achieved.' Let us hope that these words represent serious governmental intentions, and are not one more instance of easy rhetoric, quickly forgotten. In the aftermath of the American withdrawal from Vietnam, such pledges were worthless. In my view, to assure that Afghanistan will be properly remembered at an international level once the withdrawal process is completed, will depend, above all, on sustaining concern at a public level. Especially those of us who have opposed the Soviet presence must not now abandon Afghanistan and turn our attention elsewhere. Remaining vigilant, and encouraging vigilance by our governments, in the face of Soviet withdrawal may be our greatest challenge yet.

FOOTNOTES

1   M.S. Gorbachev, *Perestroika* (New York: Harper and Row, 1987) pp.176-177.
2   Eqbal Ahmad and Richard J. Barnet, 'A Reporter at Large: Bloody Games', *The New Yorker*, 11 April 1988.

10

Conclusions: Management of the Afghan Crisis

J.L. Richardson

The earlier chapters in this book demonstrate the range of issues and uncertainties which are posed by the Soviet withdrawal from Afghanistan. The interrelationships of the internal, regional and global options are exceptionally complex. There is, however, a wide measure of agreement on the initial premise that, while the Soviet commitment to withdraw constitutes a major turning point in a protracted conflict, it falls far short of a settlement or termination of that conflict.

The purpose of these concluding comments is to identify areas of agreement which emerge from the discussion, to explore some of their possible implications, and to highlight major uncertainties and differences of opinion. I have also been asked to comment on the management of the crisis, and although the concept of 'crisis management' is highly problematic, there may be something to be learned from focusing on this aspect of the Afghan conflict.[1]

If we draw the comparison with Vietnam which has arisen in several other contexts, what stands out is the relative simplicity of the 'management' problem in the earlier case, that is to say the relatively small number of the key actors and the relatively centralised character of their decision making structures. This is especially striking if the negotiation of the Paris settlement between Henry Kissinger and Le Duc Tho is contrasted with that of the Afghan Accords. In the former case the negotiators represented the governments of the principal military adversaries, which determined the outcome for their South Vietnamese clients, who themselves had no independent role in the process. The roles of the Soviet Union and China, while undoubtedly significant, remain somewhat enigmatic.

In the present instance there are far more essential actors, and their roles are more diverse and in some instances paradoxical. The Accords were negotiated at arm's length between a government highly dependent on its superpower protector (some observers would insist that it was totally dependent) and a government which informally controlled the supply of arms to the *Mujahideen* but had limited influence over their actions and represented their interests only to a limited extent. The exclusion of the *Mujahideen* from the diplomatic process, of course, points to the principal anomaly of the Accords. To construct a parallel in the Vietnamese case one would have to envisage a third party, say China, negotiating on behalf of North Vietnam with the government of South Vietnam. Such a negotiation would have held out little prospect of achieving a viable settlement.

Several of the key actors are highly decentralised. This is most obvious in the case of the *Mujahideen*, with their seven parties in exile in Peshawar, their multiplicity of local commanders, and the Shi'ite minority with its links with Iran. But it seems evident that American policy towards Afghanistan provides a rather extreme example of the Reagan Presidency's 'hands-off' style of decision making. Even though most of the story remains to be told, the prominence of bureaucratic and congressional politics is alluded to in Mr Maley's chapter and is discussed more fully in other recent publications.[2] In the case of Pakistan, although the late President Zia appears to have determined the main lines of policy, reports suggest that its implementation—in particular with respect to the transfer of arms to the *Mujahideen*—may have left a good deal of scope to Pakistan's officials to favour particular resistance groups over others or indeed to divert some of the more desirable weapons to entirely different recipients.[3] The killing of Zia opens up the possibility of new directions in Pakistan's policy during the next phase of the conflict.

Evidence relating to the management of the conflict on the Soviet side is necessarily more limited and circumstantial. It remains possible that information on divided counsels or confusion over policy implementation may eventually become available, but the accounts by three close observers in the preceding chapters suggest that the Soviet government under Gorbachev has managed the difficult task of withdrawing from an established military commitment with considerable skill, and that the political costs of withdrawal have been kept to a minimum. This was favoured by circumstances such as the increasing unpopularity of the war, by continuing tight censorship which excluded Afghanistan from the impact of *glasnost'* in other areas of Soviet life, and by prior policies such as the careful limits on the level of Soviet involvement in operations in Afghanistan, which Mr Jukes shows to have been observed from the outset. Whatever apprehensions may be felt in some leadership circles in the Soviet allies, Dr Miller shows that an ideological rationale for minimising the perception of any Afghan precedent for the crucial alliance, the Warsaw Pact, is firmly in place. Whatever the final outcome, Soviet policy up to now, in contrast to that of most other actors, shows all the indications of tight control and careful orchestration. The PDPA government in Kabul, on the other hand, never exhibited this degree of cohesion.

Which other actors are significant? Dr Saikal's chapter shows how Pakistan's role as the channel and regulator of arms supplied to the *Mujahideen* enabled it to play a central part, whereas Iran's relative isolation and its preoccupation with the war with Iraq diminished its impact on the conflict. China, initially an important source of arms and envisaged as one of the external guarantors of a settlement, became markedly less concerned over Afghanistan by the mid-1980s, as Professor Holmes shows, after its initial alarm that the invasion might foreshadow a more general expansionist phase in Soviet policy had subsided.

The setting for the next phase of the conflict, then, is highly complex. What can be said of the prospects for Afghanistan itself?

Afghanistan: The Internal Prospects

The dominant note is uncertainty. Professor Dupree outlines nine political scenarios, many of them improbable, none absolutely inconceivable; he ventures the bold projection that the best, the 'ideal' scenario, 'an Islamic Federated Republic, based on autonomous regional units', may in the end prove feasible. Dr Saikal entertains three scenarios. His preference is the same as Dupree's: as he more cautiously formulates it, 'a reasonably stable *Mujahideen*-led government'.

A prerequisite for achieving this, however, has always been the fall of the PDPA regime, possibly through internal dissension, collapse of morale, or the activities of the resistance. Would the *Mujahideen*, essentially guerrilla fighters, be able to mount offensive operations against strongly defended cities? Or deny them supplies? The questions do not answer themselves, but point towards Saikal's pessimistic, second scenario in which there is no political solution for the foreseeable future, but a protracted, 'afghanised' war. Might a renewed Soviet diplomatic offensive on behalf of a government of national reconciliation—that is, a broadening of the PDPA regime—in these circumstances find more responsive listeners in Washington or in Islamabad? And could the party leaders in Peshawar resist such pressure, whatever their inclinations might be?

Dr Saikal's third, equally pessimistic scenario, a period of political anarchy—rule by local warlords in the absence of a central government capable of establishing its legitimacy—might turn out in practice to be a variant of the second, especially if these conditions encouraged interference by external powers. Dupree rightly questions the tendency of some commentators to draw analogies with Lebanon: the solidarity of Afghan resistance to the foreign Soviet presence indeed stands in striking contrast to the Lebanese acquiescence in a Syrian or even an Israeli presence. But Saikal's third scenario points towards one of the major uncertainties facing Afghanistan: whether a state which has experienced major problems of legitimacy with respect to its central governmental institutions can overcome this problem in the next phase of its history.[4]

Dupree's optimistic scenario is premised on the assumption that the heroic sacrifices of war can provide a foundation for a

164

new legitimacy, provided the Afghans are left free to determine their own political future and provided the new central institutions leave ample scope for regional and local autonomy. He envisages a fusion of traditional, collective leadership at the local level with representatives of the new political elites including successful local military commanders. Can a pattern of pluralistic collective leadership with strong roots at the local level be translated to the centre, where the precedents for strong effective leadership are monarchical or presidential and the 'constitutional period' (1963-73) was marked by indecisive government? The prospects for the optimistic scenario depend heavily on the answer.

The Soviet Union

The chapters on the Soviet Union not only draw attention to the skill and apparent success of what might be termed a policy of damage limitation—'containing' the costs of the withdrawal from Afghanistan with respect to domestic politics, the morale and prestige of the military and the vital core of the Soviet alliance system. They also bring out that the withdrawal is in accordance with the broader rethinking of the Soviet role in the Third World, which was restricted to little-known debates among specialists under Brezhnev but has achieved substantial official acceptance under Gorbachev. A return of the Soviet troops to Kabul would run counter to a substantial body of theoretical and ideological reasoning and to the direction of Soviet policies elsewhere in the Third World.

At the same time, as Professor Rigby points out, Moscow could incur major political costs if things 'come badly unstuck in Afghanistan' from the Soviet point of view, above all if the Soviet withdrawal were to lead to the establishment of a vigorously anti-communist government there. And this in a state which was widely perceived as falling broadly within the Soviet sphere of influence before the communist seizure of power in 1978.

It is tempting to point to a nineteenth century parallel. In 1853 the Russian ambassador to Britain, Baron Brunnow, wrote to the Chancellor, Nesselrode, advising restraint in Russian policy towards the Ottoman Empire. Too forceful a policy might bring about a collapse of that Empire and/or a war against a

European coalition. Russia would benefit from restraint: a harsh treaty with Turkey would contribute nothing whatever to the reality of Russian influence. 'This was determined by the facts of the situation, not by words. Russia is strong, Turkey is weak, there is the preamble to all our treaties'.[5]

Nesselrode and Brunnow, as protagonists of a Concert of Europe approach to Russian diplomacy, could be seen as forerunners of Gorbachev, with his preference for negotiation over confrontation, but it never occurred to Nesselrode and his colleagues that Russia should refrain from exercising the influence over its weak neighbours which, in their view, its power rendered natural and inevitable. If one pursues this line of thought in relation to the present situation: the Soviet Union can afford to take a relatively relaxed stance *vis-à-vis* Afghanistan, because of its sheer weight in that part of the world. There is a network of treaties and economic agreements between the two states, many younger Afghans are Soviet-educated and the military relies heavily on Soviet training and support: surely a degree of Soviet influence must remain. But will the Soviet government take so relaxed a view of its interests, irrespective of the circumstances? Nesselrode, despite his extreme reluctance, was unable to prevent the drift of events which led to the Crimean war, a process which began when Turkey rejected what the Russian leaders were agreed in regarding as their legitimate claims.

This suggests that there will be a need for circumspection on the part of any future non-communist government of Afghanistan, and its Western and regional supporters, in defining its stance towards the Soviet Union. The worst case, from the Soviet standpoint, must be a perceived 'fundamentalist' regime in Kabul, allied to other such regimes in the region and supported by Western arms and intelligence services. It must be assumed that Moscow would be prepared to devote substantial resources to preventing such a regime from coming to power, or maintaining itself in power. Perception may be important in this regard, in view of the ambiguities that relate to 'fundamentalism'. Although Finland is often unfairly held up as a negative model (the notion of the 'finlandisation' of Europe) in fact it is a small state which fought its own war against the Soviet Union without the assistance of the great powers, and which has maintained its independence internally while respecting Soviet interests

166

externally. The record suggests that the United States is prepared to enter into only very limited relations with Afghanistan and is not prepared to place its relations with the Soviet Union at risk for the sake of that country. Thus Afghanistan's geopolitical situation is quite similar to Finland's, and while no two cases are ever identical, Finland's resolution of the dilemmas posed by proximity to a superpower might provide positive lessons for a future Kabul government. The widely-canvassed idea that a future Afghanistan should be non-aligned is a starting-point, but in a world in which states such as Pakistan, on the one hand or Cuba, on the other can claim to be non-aligned, the actual conduct of policy by Kabul, and the image it projects, are likely to be more important than protestations of non-alignment.

Normative Issues

The Geneva Accords and the choice of appropriate policies towards Afghanistan raise acute normative issues. The Accords emphasise norms of non-intervention but avoid self-determination. In strongly espousing the norm of self-determination, Professor Falk underlines the distinction between a principled policy and one of blind support for Western claims in the 'new cold war' of the 1980s. Alienated by the rhetoric of the early Reagan years, Western intellectuals have been reluctant to acknowledge that (in contrast to most other contemporary third-world conflicts) Afghanistan presents a clear case of the denial of self-determination, and that the policy of assisting the *Mujahideen* is fully justified in normative terms. The American Congress has shown a sounder perception of the ethical issues. It is true that, as Maley observes, the concept of self-determination is elusive, but clear examples of its denial, such as the present one, are readily recognised.

The more difficult problems arise with the practical application of the norm in particular cases. We may agree with Maley that in this instance it amounts to 'a process by which the empirically illegitimate regime in Kabul is replaced by one which enjoys generalised normative support'—but what kind of process? It is not conceivable that a public dismantling of a 'socialist' regime could have been written into the Accords, any more than the US could have openly abandoned South Vietnam as part of the Paris agreement in 1973. The absence of any such provisions, however—or of prior agreement, outside the framework of the Accords, on the formation of a successor government in Kabul—ensures that if self-determination is to be realised, it will be through violence, as several of the chapters recognise.

Gorbachev himself, in his speech of 9 February 1988, in effect conceded the principle, while leaving it entirely unclear how it might be implemented. The future government of Afghanistan, he said, 'is a purely internal Afghan issue. It can only be resolved by the Afghans themselves ... When it is hinted to us that the Soviet Union should take part in talks on the issue of a coalition government, or even talk to third countries, our answer is firm and clear: don't expect us to do it: it is none of our business. Or yours, for that matter.'[6] While this might be read as indicating that the art of casuistry is alive and well in Moscow, a more encouraging reading would be that it does indeed accept the principle of self-determination, and that it may signal the Soviet acceptance of the likelihood of political change in Afghanistan.

More broadly, discussion of self-determination raises the question whether there can be a genuine normative basis for East-West agreements, or only rules of convenience and prudence. In effect, if one views the present revival of detente from a Western perspective, the conflict between what Daniel Yergin called the Riga and the Yalta axioms is once more apparent.[7] On the Riga view, in its contemporary version the Reagan Doctrine, the West should be encouraged by the success of the *Mujahideen*, and the change in the Soviet stance towards the Third World more generally, to press all the more vigorously its support for anti-communist or anti-Soviet forces in other third-world trouble spots, in the name of self-determination and democratic values. On the Yalta view, this will not work: improved relations between the superpowers will require, at the very least, face-saving in the event of a serious reverse by either, respect for one another's major interests and a measure of reciprocity in their relationships.

It is misleading to depict the two approaches in terms of a contrast between principle and expediency. The contemporary version of the Riga approach is deeply flawed in that Western principles of freedom and democracy cannot be applied to ambiguous third-world trouble spots in ways which conveniently coincide with Western (or US) geopolitical interests. In some instances, as Professor Falk rightly insists, the opposite may be the case: to the extent that the norms can be made to fit the particular circumstances of Nicaragua, for example, they do not support aid to the Contras. Acknowledging this, the second approach—which needs a new name, since 'Yalta' has even less appeal than 'détente' in the American perception—would see the best hope for maximising self-determination in the present context to rest in a process of reciprocal disengagement from the politico-military involvements of the superpowers in the third world. The alternative, should Washington now follow the myopic Brezhnev precedent of the 1970s, is a predictable return to the treadmill of competing and unrewarding interventions, justified less and less convincingly by normative claims which depart ever further from reality.

The outcome in Afghanistan may well reflect certain of these wider influences. A global, universalist application of the Reagan Doctrine is likely to prompt support for 'hard-line' anti-Soviet factions in the Afghan resistance—the line favoured by the late President Zia. A policy which seeks to ease the way for Soviet acceptance of self-determination in Afghanistan, on the other hand, is likely to go along with a global policy which looks towards a reciprocal reduction in pressures for competitive intervention. There are some indications, at least, that this may be the current tendency of US policy. It is only in this way that one can envisage an early breakthrough to a political settlement in Afghanistan. The alternative Western (and *Mujahideen*) strategy points towards protracted violence and political stalemate.

Reconstruction

The problems of the reconstruction of Afghanistan's basic infrastructure—the irrigation systems, communications, the villages themselves—are daunting, always assuming that the countryside can be cleared of the mines which will otherwise create a permanent hazard for returning exiles. It is encouraging that the UN agencies have been preparing to assist, and even if the cost estimates prove to be seriously understated, the envisaged programs are well within the financial means which could reasonably be made available by the international community.

The political will to embark on such a program is quite another matter. There was no such international collaboration on behalf of Vietnam after an even longer period of warfare, and the financial plight of the UN and its agencies in the 1980s, as well as the reduced levels of development assistance to the Third World do not provide a favourable setting for the kind of ambitious program which, Professor Dupree indicates, the agencies have in mind. It may be that in the era of Gorbachev radical new departures are possible, but even so the prerequisite for any such approach will be the establishment of a government in Kabul which can exercise authority in the country as a whole. And this, as we have seen, will require political skills of a high order, on the part of the Afghans themselves and their external supporters. At a time of changing political leadership in the case of the two key Western supporters, the United States and Pakistan, this places a special responsibility on the concerned public, as Professor Falk emphasises, to ensure that the issues receive urgent attention from the new decision makers.

FOOTNOTES

1 For a general discussion of the concept, see J.L. Richardson, 'Crisis Management: A Critical Appraisal', in Gilbert R. Winham (ed.), *New Issues in International Crisis Management* (Boulder: Westview Press, 1988), pp.13-36.

2 See, for example, Rosanne Klass, 'Afghanistan: The Accords', *Foreign Affairs*, vol.66, no.5, Summer 1988, pp.922-945.

3 Edward Girardet, *Afghanistan: The Soviet War* (London: Croom Helm, 1985), pp.64-68; Radek Sikorski, 'Coda to the Russo-Afghan War: A Correspondent Reports', *Encounter*, vol.71, no.1, June 1988, pp.20-30, at p.30.

4 For a general discussion, with special reference to the PDPA government, see William Maley, 'Political Legitimation in Contemporary Afghanistan', *Asian Survey*, vol.27, no.6, June 1987, pp.705-725.

5 Norman Rich, *Why the Crimean War? A Cautionary Tale* (Hanover: University Press of New England, 1985), p.58.

6 Martin Walker, 'Gorbachev clears way for Afghanistan withdrawal', *Guardian Weekly*, 14 February 1988, p.7.

7 Daniel Yergin, *Shattered Peace: The Origins of the Cold War and the National Security State* (London: André Deutsch, 1977), pp.11, 41, 43 and *passim*.

Contributors

Louis Dupree is Adjunct Professor of Anthropology at Pennsylvania State University, and Visiting Professor in Islamic and Arabian Development Studies at Duke University. He first visited Afghanistan in 1949, and directed the Archeological Mission in Afghanistan from 1959 to 1978. He has served as consultant to UNESCO, the World Bank, the US National Security Council, and the International Rescue Committee, and his many publications include the classic work *Afghanistan* (1973).

Richard A. Falk is Albert G. Milbank Professor of International Law and Practice at Princeton University. He has appeared as counsel before the International Court of Justice on a number of occasions, and his publications include *Law, War and Morality in the Contemporary World* (1963), *The Status of Law in International Society* (1970), *A Study of Future Worlds* (1975), *Human Rights and State Sovereignty* (1981), and *Revolutionaries and Functionaries: The Dual Face of Terrorism* (1988).

Leslie Holmes is Professor of Political Science at the University of Melbourne. His works include *The Policy Process in Communist States* (1981), *Politics in the Communist World* (1986), and *Corruption and Legitimation in the Communist World* (1989). He also edited *The Withering Away of the State?* (1981), and has published widely in scholarly journals.

Geoffrey Jukes is Senior Fellow in International Relations at the Australian National University. His most recent book is *Hitler's Stalingrad Decisions* (1985), and he is currently working on Stalin's military decision-making in the Second World War. He has been a visiting scholar at Oxford and recently at the Centre of International Studies in Cambridge, and was formerly a consultant on Soviet affairs to the International Institute for Strategic Studies.

William Maley is Tutor in Politics, University College, University of New South Wales. His publications include articles in *The Modern Law Review*, *Political Studies*, *Soviet Studies*, *Asian Survey*, the *Review of International Studies*, *Australian Outlook*, and *Les Nouvelles d'Afghanistan*. He is presently investigating informal rules in the Soviet political process.

Robert F. Miller is Senior Fellow in Political Science at the Australian National University. He is author of *One Hundred Thousand Tractors: The MTS and the Development of Controls in Soviet Agriculture* (1970) and *Tito as Political Leader and External Factors in Yugoslav Political Development* (1977); and coedited (with T.H.Rigby and J.H. Miller) *Gorbachev at the Helm* (1987).

J.L. Richardson is Professorial Fellow in International Relations at the Australian National University, having previously served the same institution for over a decade as Professor of Political Science. He has also held appointments at Harvard University, Balliol College Oxford, and in the Arms Control and Disarmament Research Unit of the British Foreign Office. His publications include *Germany and the Atlantic Alliance* (1966), and his present research is focussed on international crisis diplomacy.

T.H. Rigby is Professor of Political Science at the Australian National University. He has served in the British Embassy in Moscow, and his publications include *Communist Party Membership in the USSR 1917-67* (1968), and *Lenin's Government* (1979), as well as the coedited works *Authority, Power and Policy in the USSR* (1980), *Political Legitimation in Communist States* (1982), and *Gorbachev at the Helm* (1987).

Amin Saikal is Senior Lecturer in Political Science at the Australian National University. He has been a Visiting Fellow at Princeton University, Cambridge University, and the Institute of Development Studies of the University of Sussex. He is a Rockefeller Foundation Fellow in International Relations, and his publications include *The Rise and Fall of the Shah* (1980), *The Afghanistan Conflict: Gorbachev's Options* (1987), and numerous articles in scholarly journals.

INDEX